A Day Saved
and other modern stories

A Day Saved
and other modern stories

edited by Peter Taylor

CAMBRIDGE
UNIVERSITY PRESS

CAMBRIDGE UNIVERSITY PRESS
Cambridge, New York, Melbourne, Madrid, Cape Town, Singapore,
São Paulo, Delhi, Dubai, Tokyo, Mexico City

Cambridge University Press
The Edinburgh Building, Cambridge CB2 8RU, UK

Published in the United States of America by
Cambridge University Press, New York

www.cambridge.org
Information on this title: www.cambridge.org/9780521225946

The collection, notes and questions
© Cambridge University Press 1979

First published 1979
Tenth printing 1992

A catalogue record for this publication is available from the British Library

ISBN 978-0-521-22594-6 Paperback

Contents

Preface *p.* vii

Acknowledgements *p.* viii

Ernest Hemingway: The Killers *p.* 1

Somerset Maugham: The Verger *p.* 16

Roald Dahl: The Way up to Heaven *p.* 28

H. E. Bates: Time *p.* 46

Morris Lurie: A King of the Road *p.* 55

Graham Greene: A Day Saved *p.* 67

Shiva Naipaul: A Man of Mystery *p.* 75

V. S. Pritchett: The Educated Girl *p.* 95

Murray Bail: Life of the Party *p.* 105

Frank O'Connor: The Genius *p.* 117

Preface

The stories in this book have been specially selected for advanced students of English as a foreign language. They have not been altered in any way, but can be read easily without reference to a dictionary.

A number of difficult words are marked like this*: they are explained in the glossary that comes immediately after each story. (Note that these brief explanations are intended only to help you *understand* the meaning of the words as they are used in the text; if you want to use the words yourself in other situations, you will need to get more complete information from a teacher or a good dictionary.) Some difficult words are not explained because their meaning can easily be guessed from the context, or because they are not important for a general understanding of the story.

At the beginning of each story there is a brief biographical note on the author and some suggestions to help you in selecting further stories or novels you might be interested in reading.

After each story there are some questions and topics for discussion; the questions are intended to help you see how fully you have understood the story, and the discussion topics will give you a chance to say what you think about the story and some of the issues it covers.

Above all it is hoped that you will enjoy reading these stories and that they will encourage you to read further in English.

P.J.W.T.

Acknowledgements

The editor and publishers are grateful to the following for permission to reproduce these stories:

Jonathan Cape Ltd. and the Executors of the Ernest Hemingway Estate for the use of 'The Killers'; William Heinemann Ltd. and The Estate of the late W. Somerset Maugham for the use of 'The Verger'; Roald Dahl and Murray Pollinger for the use of 'The Way up to Heaven'; Laurence Pollinger Ltd. and the Estate of the late H. E. Bates for the use of 'Time' from *The Woman who had Imagination*, published by Jonathan Cape Ltd.; Morris Lurie for the use of 'A King of the Road'; Graham Greene and Laurence Pollinger Ltd. for the use of 'A Day Saved' from *Collected Stories*, published by The Bodley Head and William Heinemann; Shiva Naipaul and Curtis Brown Ltd. for the use of 'A Man of Mystery'; V. S. Pritchett and A. D. Peters & Co. Ltd. for the use of 'The Educated Girl'; Murray Bail and University of Queensland Press for the use of 'Life of the Party' from *Contemporary Portraits and other stories*; A. D. Peters & Co. Ltd. for the use of 'The Genius'.

Ernest Hemingway
The Killers

*Hemingway was born near Chicago in 1898. During the
First World War he volunteered as an ambulance driver
on the Italian front, but was soon wounded. After the
war he returned to America where he married in 1921.
During the next few years he was a newspaper
correspondent in Europe, and his first poems and short
stories were published in Paris in 1923. He became
famous in his lifetime and many people tried to copy
his style of writing. In 1954 he was awarded the Nobel
Prize for literature and he lived most of his later life in
Cuba where he died in 1961. His best known books are*
A Farewell to Arms (*1929*), Death in the Afternoon
(*1932*), For Whom the Bell Tolls (*1940*), The Old Man
and the Sea (*1952*) *and his collection of short stories
under the title story of* The Snows of Kilimanjaro
(*1939*).

'*The Killers' is a good example of Hemingway's style:
tough language, short sentences and a high proportion
of dialogue. The surface is apparently brutal but there is
an underlying sense of compassion – particularly in the
character of Nick Adams.*

The door of Henry's lunch-room opened and two men
came in. They sat down at the counter.

'What's yours?' George asked them.

'I don't know,' one of the men said. 'What do you
want to eat, Al?'

'I don't know,' said Al. 'I don't know what I want to eat.'

Outside it was getting dark. The street-light came on outside the window. The two men at the counter read the menu. From the other end of the counter Nick Adams watched them. He had been talking to George when they came in.

'I'll have a roast pork tenderloin with apple sauce and mashed potatoes,' the first man said.

'It isn't ready yet.'

'What the hell do you put it on the card for?'

'That's the dinner,' George explained. 'You can get that at six o'clock.'

George looked at the clock on the wall behind the counter.

'It's five o'clock.'

'The clock says twenty minutes past five,' the second man said.

'It's twenty minutes fast.'

'Oh, to hell with the clock,' the first man said. 'What have you got to eat?'

'I can give you any kind of sandwiches,' George said. 'You can have ham and eggs, bacon and eggs, liver and bacon, or a steak.'

'Give me chicken croquettes with green peas and cream sauce and mashed potatoes.'

'That's the dinner.'

'Everything we want's the dinner, eh? That's the way you work it.'

'I can give you ham and eggs, bacon and eggs, liver . . .'

'I'll take ham and eggs,' the man called Al said. He wore a derby hat* and a black overcoat buttoned across the chest. His face was small and white and he had tight lips. He wore a silk muffler* and gloves.

'Give me bacon and eggs,' said the other man. He was

2

about the same size as Al. Their faces were different, but they were dressed like twins. Both wore overcoats too tight for them. They sat leaning forward, their elbows on the counter.

'Got anything to drink?' Al asked.

'Silver beer, bevo, ginger-ale,' George said.

'I mean you got anything to *drink*?'

'Just those I said.'

'This is a hot* town,' said the other. 'What do they call it?'

'Summit.'

'Ever hear of it?' Al asked his friend.

'No,' said the friend.

'What do you do here nights?' Al asked.

'They eat the dinner,' his friend said. 'They all come here and eat the big dinner.'

'That's right,' George said.

'So you think that's right?' Al asked George.

'Sure.'

'You're a pretty bright* boy, aren't you?'

'Sure,' said George.

Well, you're not,' said the other little man. 'Is he, Al?'

'He s dumb,'* said Al. He turned to Nick. 'What's your name?'

'Adams.'

'Another bright boy,' Al said. 'Ain't he a bright boy, Max?'

'The town's full of bright boys,' Max said.

George put the two platters, one of ham and eggs, the other of bacon and eggs, on the counter. He set down two side-dishes of fried potatoes and closed the wicket* into the kitchen.

'Which is yours?' he asked Al.

'Don't you remember?'

'Ham and eggs.'

3

'Just a bright boy,' Max said. He leaned forward and took the ham and eggs. Both men ate with their gloves on. George watched them eat.

'What are *you* looking at?' Max looked at George.

'Nothing.'

'The hell you were. You were looking at me.'

'Maybe the boy meant it for a joke, Max,' Al said.

George laughed.

'*You* don't have to laugh,' Max said to him. '*You* don't have to laugh at all, see?'

'All right,' said George.

'So he thinks it's all right,' Max turned to Al. 'He thinks it's all right. That's a good one.'*

'Oh, he's a thinker,' Al said. They went on eating.

'What's the bright boy's name down the counter?' Al asked Max.

'Hey, bright boy,' Max said to Nick. 'You go around on the other side of the counter with your boy friend.'

'What's the idea?' Nick asked.

'There isn't any idea.'

'You better go around, bright boy,' Al said. Nick went around behind the counter.

'What's the idea?' George asked.

'None of your damn business,' Al said. 'Who's out in the kitchen?'

'The nigger.'*

'What do you mean the nigger?'

'The nigger that cooks.'

'Tell him to come in.'

'What's the idea?'

'Tell him to come in.'

'Where do you think you are?'

'We know damn well where we are,' the man called Max said. 'Do we look silly?'*

'You talk silly,' Al said to him. 'What the hell do you

4

argue with this kid for? Listen,' he said to George, 'tell the nigger to come out here.'

'What are you going to do to him?'

'Nothing. Use your head, bright boy. What would we do to a nigger?'

George opened the slip* that opened back into the kitchen. 'Sam,' he called. 'Come in here a minute.'

The door to the kitchen opened and the nigger came in. 'What was it?' he asked. The two men at the counter took a look at him.

'All right, nigger. You stand right there,' Al said.

Sam, the nigger, standing in his apron, looked at the two men sitting at the counter. 'Yes, sir,' he said. Al got down from his stool.

'I'm going back to the kitchen with the nigger and bright boy,' he said. 'Go back to the kitchen, nigger. You go with him, bright boy.' The little man walked after Nick and Sam, the cook, back into the kitchen. The door shut after them. The man called Max sat at the counter opposite George. He didn't look at George but looked in the mirror that ran along back of the counter. Henry's had been made over* from a saloon into a lunch-counter.

'Well, bright boy,' Max said, looking into the mirror, 'why don't you say something?'

'What's it all about?'

'Hey, Al,' Max called, 'bright boy wants to know what it's all about.'

'Why don't you tell him?' Al's voice came from the kitchen.

'What do you think it's all about?'

'I don't know.'

'What do you think?'

Max looked into the mirror all the time he was talking.

'I wouldn't say.'

'Hey, Al, bright boy says he wouldn't say what he thinks it's all about.'

'I can hear you, all right,' Al said from the kitchen. He had propped open the slit that dishes passed through into the kitchen with a catsup* bottle. 'Listen, bright boy,' he said from the kitchen to George. 'Stand a little further along the bar. You move a little to the left, Max.' He was like a photographer arranging for a group picture.

'Talk to me, bright boy,' Max said. 'What do you think's going to happen?'

George did not say anything.

'I'll tell you,' Max said. 'We're going to kill a Swede. Do you know a big Swede named Ole Andreson?'

'Yes.'

'He comes here to eat every night, don't he?'

'Sometimes he comes here.'

'He comes here at six o'clock, don't he?'

'If he comes.'

'We know all that, bright boy,' Max said. 'Talk about something else. Ever go to the movies?'*

'Once in a while.'

'You ought to go to the movies more. The movies are fine for a bright boy like you.'

'What are you going to kill Ole Andreson for? What did he ever do to you?'

'He never had a chance to do anything to us. He never even seen us.'

'And he's only going to see us once,' Al said from the kitchen.

'What are you going to kill him for, then?' George asked.

'We're killing him for a friend. Just to oblige a friend, bright boy.'

'Shut up,' said Al from the kitchen. 'You talk too god-damn much.'

6

'Well, I got to keep bright boy amused. Don't I, bright boy?'

'You talk too damn much,' Al said. 'The nigger and my bright boy are amused by themselves. I got them tied up like a couple of girl friends in the convent.'

'I suppose you were in a convent.'

'You never know.'

'You were in a kosher* convent. That's where you were.'

George looked up at the clock.

'If anybody comes in you tell them the cook is off,* and if they keep after it, you tell them you'll go back and cook yourself. Do you get that, bright boy?'

'All right,' George said. 'What you going to do with us afterwards?'

'That'll depend,' Max said. 'That's one of those things you never know at the time.'

George looked up at the clock. It was a quarter past six. The door from the street opened. A street-car motorman came in.

'Hello, George,' he said. 'Can I get supper?'

'Sam's gone out,' George said. 'He'll be back in about half-an-hour.'

'I'd better go up the street,' the motorman said. George looked at the clock. It was twenty minutes past six.

'That was nice, bright boy,' Max said. 'You're a regular little gentleman.'

'He knew I'd blow his head off,' Al said from the kitchen.

'No,' said Max. 'It ain't that. Bright boy is nice. He's a nice boy. I like him.'

At six-fifty-five George said: 'He's not coming.'

Two other people had been in the lunch-room. Once George had gone out to the kitchen and made a ham-and-egg sandwich 'to go' that a man wanted to take with him. Inside the kitchen he saw Al, his derby hat tipped back, sitting on a stool beside the wicket with the muzzle of a sawed-off shotgun resting on the ledge. Nick and the cook were back to back in the corner, a towel tied in each of their mouths. George had cooked the sandwich, wrapped it up in oiled paper, put it in a bag, brought it in, and the man had paid for it and gone out.

'Bright boy can do everything,' Max said. 'He can cook and everything. You'd make some girl a nice wife, bright boy.'

'Yes?' George said. 'Your friend, Ole Andreson, isn't going to come.'

'We'll give him ten minutes,' Max said.

Max watched the mirror and the clock. The hands of the clock marked seven o'clock, and then five minutes past seven.

'Come on, Al,' said Max. 'We better go. He's not coming.'

'Better give him five minutes,' Al said from the kitchen.

In the five minutes a man came in, and George explained that the cook was sick.

'Why the hell don't you get another cook?' the man asked. 'Aren't you running a lunch-counter?' He went out.

'Come on, Al,' Max said.

'What about the two bright boys and the nigger?'

'They're all right.'

'You think so?'

'Sure. We're through* with it.'

'I don't like it,' said Al. 'It's sloppy.* You talk too much.'

'Oh, what the hell,' said Max. 'We got to keep amused, haven't we?'

'You talk too much, all the same,' Al said. He came out from the kitchen. The cut-off barrels of the shotgun

8

made a slight bulge under the waist of his too tight-fitting overcoat. He straightened his coat with his gloved hands.

'So long,* bright boy,' he said to George. 'You got a lot of luck.'

'That's the truth,' Max said. 'You ought to play the races,* bright boy.'

The two of them went out the door. George watched them, through the window, pass under the arc-light and cross the street. In their tight overcoats and derby hats they looked like a vaudeville* team. George went back through the swinging-door into the kitchen and untied Nick and the cook.

'I don't want any more of that,' said Sam, the cook. 'I don't want any more of that.'

Nick stood up. He had never had a towel in his mouth before.

'Say,' he said. 'What the hell?' He was trying to swagger it off.*

'They were going to kill Ole Andreson,' George said. 'They were going to shoot him when he came in to eat.'

'Ole Andreson?'

'Sure.'

The cook felt the corners of his mouth with his thumbs.

'They all gone?' he asked.

'Yeah,' said George. 'They're gone now.'

'I don't like it,' said the cook. 'I don't like any of it at all.'

'Listen,' George said to Nick. 'You better go see Ole Andreson.'

'All right.'

'You better not have anything to do with it at all,' Sam, the cook said. 'You better stay way out of it.'

'Don't go if you don't want to,' George said.

'Mixing up in this ain't going to get you anywhere,' the cook said. 'You stay out of it.'

'I'll go see him,' Nick said to George. 'Where does he live?'

The cook turned away.

'Little boys always know what they want to do,' he said.

'He lives up at Hirsch's rooming-house,' George said to Nick.

'I'll go up there.'

Outside, the arc-light shone through the bare branches of a tree. Nick walked up the street beside the car-tracks and turned at the next arc-light down a side-street. Three houses up the street was Hirsch's rooming-house. Nick walked up the two steps and pushed the bell. A woman came to the door.

'Is Ole Andreson here?'

'Do you want to see him?'

'Yes, if he's in.'

Nick followed the woman up a flight of stairs and back to the end of the corridor. She knocked on the door.

'Who is it?'

'It's somebody to see you, Mr Andreson,' the woman said.

'It's Nick Adams.'

'Come in.'

Nick opened the door and went into the room. Ole Andreson was lying on the bed with all his clothes on. He had been a heavyweight prizefighter* and he was too long for the bed. He lay with his head on two pillows. He did not look at Nick.

'What was it?' he asked.

'I was up at Henry's,' Nick said, 'and two fellows came in and tied up me and the cook, and they said they were going to kill you.'

It sounded silly when he said it. Ole Andreson said nothing.

'They put us out in the kitchen,' Nick went on. 'They were going to shoot you when you came in to supper.'

Ole Andreson looked at the wall and did not say anything.

'George thought I better come and tell you about it.'

'There isn't anything I can do about it,' Ole Andreson said.

'I'll tell you what they were like.'

'I don't want to know what they were like,' Ole Andreson said. He looked at the wall. 'Thanks for coming to tell me about it.'

'That's all right.'

Nick looked at the big man lying on the bed.

'Don't you want me to go and see the police?'

'No,' Ole Andreson said. 'That wouldn't do any good.'

'Isn't there something I could do?'

'No. There ain't anything to do.'

'Maybe it was just a bluff.'*

'No. It ain't just a bluff.'

Ole Andreson rolled over towards the wall.

'The only thing is,' he said, talking towards the wall, 'I just can't make up my mind to go out. I been in here all day.'

'Couldn't you get out of town?'

'No,' Ole Andreson said, 'I'm through with all that running around.'

He looked at the wall.

'There ain't anything to do now.'

'Couldn't you fix it up* some way?'

'No. I got in wrong.'* He talked in the same flat voice. 'There ain't anything to do. After a while I'll make up my mind to go out.'

'I better go back and see George,' Nick said.

'So long,' said Ole Andreson. He did not look towards Nick. 'Thanks for coming around.'

Nick went out. As he shut the door he saw Ole Andreson with all his clothes on, lying on the bed looking at the wall.

'He's been in his room all day,' the landlady said downstairs. 'I guess he don't feel well. I said to him: "Mr Andreson, you ought to go out and take a walk on a nice fall* day like this," but he didn't feel like it.'

'He doesn't want to go out.'

'I'm sorry he don't feel well,' the woman said. 'He's an awfully nice man. He was in the ring,* you know.'

'I know it.'

'You'd never know it except for the way his face is,' the woman said. They stood talking just inside the street door. 'He's just as gentle.'

'Well, good night, Mrs Hirsch,' Nick said.

'I'm not Mrs Hirsch,' the woman said. 'She owns the place. I just look after it for her. I'm Mrs Bell.'

'Well, good night, Mrs Bell,' Nick said.

'Good night,' the woman said.

Nick walked up the dark street to the corner under the arc-light, and then along the car-tracks to Henry's eating-house. George was inside, back of the counter.

'Did you see Ole?'

'Yes,' said Nick. 'He's in his room and he won't go out.'

The cook opened the door from the kitchen when he heard Nick's voice.

'I don't even listen to it,' he said and shut the door.

'Did you tell him about it?' George asked.

'Sure. I told him, but he knows what it's all about.'

'What's he going to do?'

'Nothing.'

'They'll kill him.'

'I guess they will.'

'He must have got mixed up in something in Chicago.'

'I guess so,' said Nick.

'It's a hell of a thing.'

'It's an awful thing,' Nick said.

They did not say anything. George reached down for a towel and wiped the counter.

'I wonder what he did?' Nick said.

'Double-crossed* somebody. That's what they kill them for.'

'I'm going to get out of this town,' Nick said.

'Yes,' said George. 'That's a good thing to do.'

'I can't stand to think about him waiting in the room and knowing he's going to get it.* It's too damned awful.'

'Well,' said George, 'you better not think about it.'

Glossary

page 2
derby hat: stiff, felt hat
muffler: thick, warm scarf

page 3
hot: exciting, lively
bright: intelligent
dumb: stupid
wicket: small door or gate

page 4
a good one: something very amusing
nigger (slang): negro
silly: stupid, crazy

page 5
slip: the opening through which food is passed from the
    kitchen
made over: converted

Ernest Hemingway

page 6
catsup: (= ketchup) tomato sauce
movies: cinema, films

page 7
kosher: Jewish
off: not on duty, not there

page 8
through: finished
sloppy: inefficient, unprofessional

page 9
so long: goodbye
play the races: put money on horses in races
vaudeville: variety entertainment
to swagger it off: (to pretend) to be brave and unafraid as if
    nothing had happened.

page 10
prizefighter: professional boxer

page 11
bluff: deliberate and boastful pretence
fix it up: come to some agreement
got in wrong: became involved with a group of bad people

page 12
fall (American): autumn
in the ring: a boxer (who fought in a boxing ring)

page 13
double-crossed: cheated, betrayed
get it: be killed

Questions

1 What does one of the killers mean when he says:
  'Everything we want's the dinner, eh? That's the way you
  work it' (page 2)?

14

2 What is George's job?
3 How long do Al and Max wait in the lunch-room before they decide to leave?
4 What differences do you notice between Al and Max?
5 Why does Al become increasingly annoyed with his partner Max?
6 In what ways is Nick Adams unlike George and Sam?
7 Describe Ole Andreson as completely as you can.

Topics for discussion

1 From information in the story try and build up as full a picture of Summit as you can.
2 Why do you think Al and Max have been sent to kill Ole Andreson?
3 What would you have done if George had asked you to go and tell Ole Andreson what had happened in the lunch-room?
4 On page 10 Sam the cooks says, 'Little boys always know what they want to do.' How far is this true?
5 Why do you think Ole Andreson refused Nick's offer of help?
6 How far do you agree with George's final remark, 'You better not think about it' (page 13)
7 Do you think Nick would follow George's advice? Give your reasons.

Somerset Maugham
The Verger*

*Somerset Maugham was born in Paris in 1874 and spent
his early childhood there. Later he studied medicine in
London, but the success of his first novel,* Liza of
Lambeth *(1897), made him decide to devote his life to
writing instead. In the 1930s and 40s he had
considerable success as a playwright, and also became
increasingly well known as a novelist and writer of short
stories and travel books. After 1930 he lived mostly in
the south of France, where he died in 1965. Among his
best known novels are* Of Human Bondage *(1915),* The
Painted Veil *(1925), and his last major novel,* The
Razor's Edge *(1944).*

*The story of 'The Verger' tells the sympathetic tale of
a man, who although unable to read or write, becomes
very successful guided only by his personal pride and
firm sense of purpose.*

There had been a christening that afternoon at St
Peter's, Neville Square, and Albert Edward Foreman
still wore his verger's gown. He kept his new one, its
folds as full and stiff as though it were made not of alpaca* but of perennial bronze, for funerals and weddings
(St Peter's, Neville Square, was a church much favoured
by the fashionable for these ceremonies) and now he
wore only his second-best. He wore it with complacence,
for it was the dignified symbol of his office, and without
it (when he took it off to go home) he had the discon-

certing sensation of being somewhat insufficiently clad.*
He took pains* with it; he pressed it and ironed it himself. During the sixteen years he had been verger of this
church he had had a succession of such gowns, but he
had never been able to throw them away when they
were worn out and the complete series, neatly
wrapped up in brown paper, lay in the bottom drawers
of the wardrobe in his bedroom.

The verger busied himself quietly, replacing the
painted wooden cover on the marble font, taking away a
chair that had been brought for an infirm old lady, and
waited for the vicar* to have finished in the vestry* so
that he could tidy up in there and go home. Presently he
saw him walk across the chancel, genuflect in front of
the high altar, and come down the aisle; but he still
wore his cassock.

'What's he 'anging about* for?' the verger said to
himself. 'Don't 'e know* I want my tea?'

The vicar had been but recently appointed, a red-
faced energetic man in the early forties, and Albert
Edward still regretted his predecessor, a clergyman of
the old school who preached leisurely sermons in a sil-
very voice and dined out a great deal with his more
aristocratic parishioners. He liked things in church to be
just so,* but he never fussed; he was not like this new
man who wanted to have his finger in every pie.* But
Albert Edward was tolerant. St Peter's was in a very
good neighbourhood and the parishioners were a very nice
class of people. The new vicar had come from the
East End* and he couldn't be expected to fall in* all
at once with the discreet ways of his fashionable congregation.

'All this 'ustle,'* said Albert Edward. 'But give 'im
time, he'll learn.'

When the vicar had walked down the aisle so far that
he could address the verger without raising his voice

more than was becoming in a place of worship he stopped.

'Foreman, will you come into the vestry for a minute. I have something to say to you.'

'Very good, sir.'

The vicar waited for him to come up and they walked up the church together.

'A very nice christening, I thought, sir. Funny 'ow the baby stopped cryin' the moment you took him.'

'I've noticed they very often do,' said the vicar, with a little smile. 'After all I've had a good deal of practice with them.'

It was a source of subdued pride to him that he could nearly always quiet a whimpering infant by the manner in which he held it and he was not unconscious of the amused admiration with which mothers and nurses watched him settle the baby in the crook of his surpliced arm. The verger knew that it pleased him to be complimented on his talent.

The vicar preceded Albert Edward into the vestry. Albert Edward was a trifle* surprised to find the two churchwardens* there. He had not seen them come in. They gave him pleasant nods.

'Good afternoon, my lord. Good afternoon, sir,' he said to one after the other.

They were elderly men, both of them, and they had been church-wardens almost as long as Albert Edward had been verger. They were sitting now at a handsome refectory table that the old vicar had brought many years before from Italy and the vicar sat down in the vacant chair between them. Albert Edward faced them, the table between him and them, and wondered with slight uneasiness what was the matter. He remembered still the occasion on which the organist had got into trouble and the bother they had all had to hush things up.* In a church like St Peter's, Neville Square, they couldn't afford a scandal. On the vicar's red face was a look of resolute benignity,* but the others bore an expression that was slightly troubled.

'He's been naggin'* them, he 'as,' said the verger to himself. 'He's jockeyed* them into doin' something, but they don't 'alf like* it. That's what it is, you mark my words.'

But his thoughts did not appear on Albert Edward's clean-cut and distinguished features. He stood in a respectful but not obsequious attitude. He had been in service before he was appointed to his ecclesiastical office, but only in very good houses, and his deportment was irreproachable. Starting as a page-boy in the household of a merchant-prince, he had risen by due degrees from the position of fourth to first footman,* for a year he had been single-handed butler to a widowed peeress,* and, till the vacancy occurred at St Peter's, butler with two men under him in the house of a retired ambassador. He was tall, spare, grave, and dignified. He looked, if not like a duke, at least like an actor of the old school who specialized in dukes' parts. He had tact, firmness, and self-assurance. His character was unimpeachable.

The vicar began briskly.

'Foreman, we've got something rather unpleasant to say to you. You've been here a great many years and I think his lordship and the general agree with me that you've fulfilled the duties of your office to the satisfaction of everybody concerned.'

The two churchwardens nodded.

'But a most extraordinary circumstance came to my knowledge the other day and I felt it my duty to impart it to the church-wardens. I discovered to my astonishment that you could neither read nor write.'

The verger's face betrayed no sign of embarrassment.

'The last vicar knew that, sir,' he replied. 'He said it

didn't make no difference. He always said there was a great deal too much education in the world for 'is taste.'

'It's the most amazing thing I ever heard,' cried the general. 'Do you mean to say that you've been verger of this church for sixteen years and never learned to read or write?'

'I went into service when I was twelve, sir. The cook in the first place tried to teach me once, but I didn't seem to 'ave the knack* for it, and then what with one thing and another I never seemed to 'ave the time. I've never really found the want of it. I think a lot of these young fellows waste a rare lot of time readin' when they might be doin' something useful.'

'But don't you want to know the news?' said the other churchwarden. 'Don't you ever want to write a letter?'

'No, me lord, I seem to manage very well without. And of late years now they've all these pictures in the papers I get to know what's goin' on pretty well. Me wife's quite a scholar and if I want to write a letter she writes it for me. It's not as if I was a bettin' man.'*

The two churchwardens gave the vicar a troubled glance and then looked down at the table.

'Well, Foreman, I've talked the matter over with these gentlemen and they quite agree with me that the situation is impossible. At a church like St Peter's, Neville Square, we cannot have a verger who can neither read nor write.'

Albert Edward's thin, sallow face reddened and he moved uneasily on his feet, but he made no reply.

'Understand me, Foreman, I have no complaint to make against you. You do your work quite satisfactorily; I have the highest opinion both of your character and of your capacity; but we haven't the right to take the risk of some accident that might happen owing to your lamentable ignorance. It's a matter of prudence as well as of principle.'

'But couldn't you learn, Foreman?' asked the general.

'No, sir, I'm afraid I couldn't, not now. You see, I'm not as young as I was and if I couldn't seem able to get the letters in me 'ead when I was a nipper* I don't think there's much chance of it now.'

'We don't want to be harsh with you, Foreman,' said the vicar. 'But the churchwardens and I have quite made up our minds. We'll give you three months and if at the end of that time you cannot read and write I'm afraid you'll have to go.'

Albert Edward had never liked the new vicar. He'd said from the beginning that they'd made a mistake when they gave him St Peter's. He wasn't the type of man they wanted with a classy* congregation like that. And now he straightened himself a little. He knew his value and he wasn't going to allow himself to be put upon.*

'I'm very sorry, sir, I'm afraid it's no good. I'm too old a dog to learn new tricks. I've lived a good many years without knowin' 'ow to read and write, and without wishin' to praise myself, self-praise is no recommendation, I don't mind sayin' I've done my duty in that state of life in which it 'as pleased a merciful providence to place me, and if I *could* learn now I don't know as I'd want to.'

'In that case, Foreman, I'm afraid you must go.'

'Yes, sir, I quite understand. I shall be 'appy to 'and in my resignation as soon as you've found somebody to take my place.'

But when Albert Edward with his usual politeness had closed the church door behind the vicar and the two churchwardens he could not sustain the air of unruffled dignity with which he had borne the blow inflicted upon him and his lips quivered. He walked slowly back to the vestry and hung up on its proper peg his verger's gown. He sighed as he thought of all the grand funerals and smart weddings it had seen. He tidied everything up, put on his coat, and hat in hand walked down the aisle. He locked the church door behind him. He strolled across the square, but deep in his sad thoughts he did not take the street that led him home, where a nice strong cup of tea awaited him; he took the wrong turning. He walked slowly along. His heart was heavy. He did not know what he should do with himself. He did not fancy* the notion of going back to domestic service; after being his own master for so many years, for the vicar and churchwardens could say what they liked, it was he that had run* St Peter's, Neville Square, he could scarcely demean* himself by accepting a situation.* He had saved a tidy sum,* but not enough to live on without doing something, and life seemed to cost more every year. He had never thought to be troubled with such questions. The vergers of St Peter's, like the popes of Rome, were there for life. He had often thought of the pleasant reference the vicar would make in his sermon at evensong the first Sunday after his death to the long and faithful service, and the exemplary character of their late verger, Albert Edward Foreman. He sighed deeply. Albert Edward was a nonsmoker and a total abstainer, but with a certain latitude; that is to say he liked a glass of beer with his dinner and when he was tired he enjoyed a cigarette. It occurred to him now that one would comfort him and since he did not carry them he looked about him for a shop where he could buy a packet of Gold Flakes. He did not at once see one and walked on a little. It was a long street, with all sorts of shops in it, but there was not a single one where you could buy cigarettes.

'That's strange,' said Albert Edward.

To make sure he walked right up the street again. No, there was no doubt about it. He stopped and looked reflectively up and down.

'I can't be the only man as walks along this street and wants a fag,'* he said. 'I shouldn't wonder but what a fellow might do very well with a little shop here. Tobacco and sweets, you know.'

He gave a sudden start.

'That's an idea,' he said. 'Strange 'ow things come to you when you least expect it.'

He turned, walked home, and had his tea.

'You're very silent this afternoon, Albert,' his wife remarked.

'I'm thinkin',' he said.

He considered the matter from every point of view and next day he went along the street and by good luck found a little shop to let* that looked as though it would exactly suit him. Twenty-four hours later he had taken it, and when a month after that he left St Peter's, Neville Square, for ever, Albert Edward Foreman set up in business as a tobacconist and newsagent. His wife said it was a dreadful come-down* after being verger of St Peter's, but he answered that you had to move with the times, the church wasn't what it was, and 'enceforeward he was going to render unto Caesar what was Caesar's.* Albert Edward did very well. He did so well that in a year or so it struck him that he might take a second shop and put a manager in. He looked for another long street that hadn't got a tobacconist in it and when he found it, and a shop to let, took it and stocked it. This was a success too. Then it occurred to him that if he could run two he could run half a dozen, so he began walking about London, and whenever he found a long street that had no tobacconist and a shop to let he took it. In the course of ten years he had acquired no less than ten shops and he was making money hand over fist.* He went round to all of them himself every Monday, collected the week's takings, and took them to the bank.

One morning when he was there paying in a bundle

of notes and a heavy bag of silver the cashier told him that the manager would like to see him. He was shown into an office and the manager shook hands with him.

'Mr Foreman, I wanted to have a talk to you about the money you've got on deposit with us. D'you know exactly how much it is?'

'Not within a pound or two, sir; but I've got a pretty rough* idea.'

'Apart from what you paid in this morning it's a little over thirty thousand pounds. That's a very large sum to have on deposit and I should have thought you'd do better to invest it.'

'I wouldn't want to take no risk, sir. I know it's safe in the bank.'

'You needn't have the least anxiety. We'll make you out a list of absolutely gilt-edged securities.* They'll bring you in a better rate of interest than we can possibly afford to give you.'

A troubled look settled on Mr Foreman's distinguished face. 'I've never 'ad anything to do with stocks and shares and I'd 'ave to leave it all in your 'ands,' he said.

The manager smiled. 'We'll do everything. All you'll have to do next time you come in is just to sign the transfers.'

'I could do that all right,' said Albert uncertainly. 'But 'ow should I know what I was signin'?'

'I suppose you can read,' said the manager a trifle sharply.

Mr Foreman gave him a disarming smile.

'Well, sir, that's just it. I can't. I know it sounds funny-like, but there it is, I can't read or write, only me name, an' I only learnt to do that when I went into business.'

The manager was so surprised that he jumped up from his chair.

24

'That's the most extraordinary thing I ever heard.'

'You see, it's like this, sir, I never 'ad the opportunity until it was too late and then some'ow I wouldn't. I got obstinate-like.'

The manager stared at him as though he were a prehistoric monster.

'And do you mean to say that you've built up this important business and amassed a fortune of thirty thousand pounds without being able to read or write? Good God, man, what would you be now if you had been able to?'

'I can tell you that, sir,' said Mr Foreman, a little smile on his still aristocratic features. 'I'd be verger of St Peter's, Neville Square.'

Glossary

page 16
verger: the official whose job is to look after the interior of a church
alpaca: cloth made from long, fine animal hair

page 17
clad: clothed, dressed
took pains: was very careful
vicar: priest in the church
vestry: place where the ecclesiastical robes are kept in a church
'anging about: (= hanging about) waiting
don't 'e know: (= doesn't he know)
just so: absolutely correct and in order
to have his finger in every pie: to be personally involved (almost to the point of interfering) in everything
East End: Eastern and poorer part of London
fall in: accept, understand
'ustle: (= hustle) hurried, noisy activity

page 18
trifle: a little bit

Somerset Maugham

churchwardens: non-ecclesiastical (or lay) assistants to the
    priest
hush things up: keep the truth about something from the
    general public

page 19
benignity: kindness
naggin' (= nagging): constantly bothering, annoying someone
jockeyed: manoeuvred (like a jockey controlling a racehorse)
don't 'alf like it: (= don't half like it) don't like it at all
footman: manservant
peeress: a female peer, someone who has a seat in the House of
    Lords (the Upper House in the English Parliament)

page 20
knack: talent, aptitude
bettin' man: (= betting man) someone who puts money on the
    result of something uncertain (like a horserace)

page 21
nipper: (slang) small boy
classy: upper class, aristocratic
put upon: treated badly because of his lack of education

page 22
fancy: like, feel attracted by
run: organised
demean: humiliate
situation: a job in domestic service
a tidy sum: quite a lot of money

page 23
fag: (slang) cigarette
to let: to rent, pay money for the use of the shop
come-down: drop in social status, a change for the worse
to render unto Caesar what was Caesar's: (taken from
    the gospels in the Bible) one should not try to put
    different things into the same category
hand over fist: in huge amounts very fast

page 24
pretty rough: reasonably accurate
gilt-edged securities: safe investments

Questions

1 What did the verger dislike about the new vicar of St Peter's, Neville Square?
2 In what ways did Albert Edward think the new vicar was unsuitable for his post?
3 What indications are there that Albert Edward took great pride in his position as verger of St Peter's?
4 Why did the vicar and the churchwardens feel it was necessary to dismiss Albert Edward?
5 What was Albert Edward's reaction to his dismissal?
6 Did you find his reaction surprising in any way?
7 Why was Albert Edward's wife unhappy about him starting his own business?
8 Describe the main good qualities of Albert Edward as a person

Topics for discussion

1 How far do you think the vicar and the churchwardens were justified in their decision to dismiss Albert Edward?
2 To what extent do you feel Albert Edward was right in his refusal to learn to read and write?
3 How would you have reacted in his situation?
4 Describe some self-made man you know personally or have heard about.
5 How does the author show his sympathy for Albert Edward?
6 To what extent did luck play a part in Albert Edward's success?
7 How important do you think a formal education is?
8 What particular aspects of the story did you like (or dislike)?

Roald Dahl
The Way up to Heaven

*Although Roald Dahl's parents were Norwegian, he was
brought up in England and has always written in
English. He has led a varied and active life, and began
writing while he was in the U.S.A. during the Second
World War. He has concentrated on short stories, many
of them like this one involving a bizarre twist of events.
Among his best known collections are* Over To You
(*1945*), Someone Like You (*1953*), Kiss Kiss (*1959*) *and*
Switch Bitch (*1974*). *He has also had great success as a
writer of children's books.*

*In this particular story we see how a woman gets
revenge on her husband with frightening finality.*

All her life, Mrs Foster had had an almost pathological
fear of missing a train, a plane, a boat, or even a theatre
curtain.* In other respects, she was not a particularly
nervous woman, but the mere thought of being late on
occasions like these would throw her into such a state of
nerves that she would begin to twitch. It was nothing
much – just a tiny vellicating muscle in the corner of the
left eye, like a secret wink – but the annoying thing was
that it refused to disappear until an hour or so after the
train or plane or whatever it was had been safely caught.

It was really extraordinary how in certain people a
simple apprehension about a thing like catching a train
can grow into a serious obsession. At least an hour
before it was time to leave the house for the station, Mrs
Foster would step out of the elevator all ready to go,

28

with hat and coat and gloves, and then, being quite unable to sit down, she would flutter and fidget about from room to room until her husband, who must have been well aware of her state, finally emerged from his privacy and suggested in a cool dry voice that perhaps they had better get going now, had they not?

Mr Foster may possibly have had a right to be irritated by this foolishness of his wife's, but he could have had no excuse for increasing her misery by keeping her waiting unnecessarily. Mind you, it is by no means certain that this is what he did, yet whenever they were to go somewhere, his timing was so accurate – just a minute or two late, you understand – and his manner so bland that it was hard to believe he wasn't purposely inflicting a nasty private little torture of his own on the unhappy lady. And one thing he must have known – that she would never dare to call out and tell him to hurry. He had disciplined her too well for that. He must also have known that if he was prepared to wait even beyond the last moment of safety, he could drive her nearly into hysterics. On one or two special occasions in the later years of their married life, it seemed almost as though he had *wanted* to miss the train simply in order to intensify the poor woman's suffering.

Assuming (though one cannot be sure) that the husband was guilty, what made his attitude doubly unreasonable was the fact that, with the exception of this one small irrepressible foible,* Mrs Foster was and always had been a good and loving wife. For over thirty years, she had served him loyally and well. There was no doubt about this. Even she, a very modest woman, was aware of it, and although she had for years refused to let herself believe that Mr Foster would ever consciously torment her, there had been times recently when she had caught herself beginning to wonder.

Mr Eugene Foster, who was nearly seventy years old,

lived with his wife in a large six-storey house in New York City, on East Sixty-second Street, and they had four servants. It was a gloomy place, and few people came to visit them. But on this particular morning in January, the house had come alive and there was a great deal of bustling about. One maid was distributing bundles of dust sheets to every room, while another was draping them over the furniture. The butler was bringing down suitcases and putting them in the hall. The cook kept popping up from the kitchen to have a word with the butler, and Mrs Foster herself, in an old-fashioned fur coat and with a black hat on the top of her head, was flying from room to room and pretending to supervise these operations. Actually, she was thinking of nothing at all except that she was going to miss her plane if her husband didn't come out of his study soon and get ready.

'What time is it, Walker?' she said to the butler as she passed him.

'It's ten minutes past nine, Madam.'

'And has the car come?'

'Yes, Madam, it's waiting. I'm just going to put the luggage in now.'

'It takes an hour to get to Idlewild,'* she said. 'My plane leaves at eleven. I have to be there half an hour beforehand for the formalities. I shall be late. I just *know* I'm going to be late.'

'I think you have plenty of time, Madam,' the butler said kindly. 'I warned Mr Foster that you must leave at nine-fifteen. There's still another five minutes.'

'Yes, Walker, I know, I know. But get the luggage in quickly, will you please?'

She began walking up and down the hall, and whenever the butler came by, she asked him the time. This, she kept telling herself, was the *one* plane she must not miss. It had taken months to persuade her husband to allow her to go. If she missed it, he might easily decide that she should cancel the whole thing. And the trouble was that he insisted on coming to the airport to see her off.

'Dear God,' she said aloud, 'I'm going to miss it. I know, I know, I *know* I'm going to miss it.' The little muscle beside the left eye was twitching madly now. The eyes themselves were very close to tears.

'What time is it, Walker?'

'It's eighteen minutes past, Madam.'

'Now I really *will* miss it!' she cried. 'Oh, I wish he would come!'

This was an important journey for Mrs Foster. She was going all alone to Paris to visit her daughter, her only child, who was married to a Frenchman. Mrs Foster didn't care much for the Frenchman, but she was fond of her daughter, and, more than that, she had developed a great yearning to set eyes on her three grand-children. She knew them only from the many photographs that she had received and that she kept putting up all over the house. They were beautiful, these children. She doted on them, and each time a new picture arrived she would carry it away and sit with it for a long time, staring at it lovingly and searching the small faces for signs of that old satisfying blood likeness that meant so much. And now, lately, she had come more and more to feel that she did not really wish to live out her days in a place where she could not be near these children, and have them visit her, and take them for walks, and buy them presents, and watch them grow. She knew, of course, that it was wrong and in a way disloyal to have thoughts like these while her husband was still alive. She knew also that although he was no longer active in his many enterprises, he would never consent to leave New York and live in Paris. It was a miracle that he had ever agreed to let her fly over there

31

alone for six weeks to visit them. But, oh, how she wished she could live there always, and be close to them!

'Walker, what time is it?'

'Twenty-two minutes past, Madam.'

As he spoke, a door opened and Mr Foster came into the hall. He stood for a moment, looking intently at his wife, and she looked back at him – at this diminutive but still quite dapper* old man with the huge bearded face that bore such an astonishing resemblance to those old photographs of Andrew Carnegie.*

'Well,' he said, 'I suppose perhaps we'd better get going fairly soon if you want to catch that plane.'

'*Yes,* dear – *yes!* Everything's ready. The car's waiting.'

'That's good,' he said. With his head over to one side, he was watching her closely. He had a peculiar way of cocking the head and then moving it in a series of small, rapid jerks. Because of this and because he was clasping his hands up high in front of him, near the chest, he was somehow like a squirrel standing there – a quick clever old squirrel from the Park.*

'Here's Walker with your coat, dear. Put it on.'

'I'll be with you in a moment,' he said. 'I'm just going to wash my hands.'

She waited for him, and the tall butler stood beside her, holding the coat and the hat.

'Walker, will I miss it?'

'No, Madam,' the butler said. 'I think you'll make it all right.'

Then Mr Foster appeared again, and the butler helped him on with his coat. Mrs Foster hurried outside and got into the hired Cadillac. Her husband came after her, but he walked down the steps of the house slowly, pausing halfway to observe the sky and to sniff the cold morning air.

'It looks a bit foggy,' he said as he sat down beside her in the car. 'And it's always worse out there at the airport. I shouldn't be surprised if the flight's cancelled already.'

'Don't say that, dear – *please.*'

They didn't speak again until the car had crossed over the river to Long Island.

'I arranged everything with the servants,' Mr Foster said. 'They're all going off today. I gave them half-pay for six weeks and told Walker I'd send him a telegram when we wanted them back.'

'Yes,' she said. 'He told me.'

'I'll move into the club* tonight. It'll be a nice change staying at the club.'

'Yes, dear. I'll write to you.'

'I'll call in at the house occasionally to see that everything's all right and to pick up the mail.'

'But don't you really think Walker should stay there all the time to look after things?' she asked meekly.

'Nonsense. It's quite unnecessary. And anyway, I'd have to pay him full wages.'

'Oh yes,' she said. 'Of course.'

'What's more, you never know what people get up to when they're left alone in a house,' Mr Foster announced, and with that he took out a cigar and, after snipping off the end with a silver cutter, lit it with a gold lighter.

She sat still in the car with her hands clasped together tight under the rug.

'Will you write to me?' she asked.

'I'll see,' he said. 'But I doubt it. You know I don't hold with* letter-writing unless there's something specific to say.'

'Yes, dear, I know. So don't you bother.'

They drove on, along Queen's Boulevard, and as they

approached the flat marshland on which Idlewild is built, the fog began to thicken and the car had to slow down.

'Oh dear!' cried Mrs Foster. 'I'm *sure* I'm going to miss it now! What time is it?'

'Stop fussing,' the old man said. 'It doesn't matter anyway. It's bound to be cancelled now. They never fly in this sort of weather. I don't know why you bothered to come out.'

She couldn't be sure, but it seemed to her that there was suddenly a new note in his voice, and she turned to look at him. It was difficult to observe any change in his expression under all that hair. The mouth was what counted. She wished, as she had so often before, that she could see the mouth clearly. The eyes never showed anything except when he was in a rage.

'Of course,' he went on, 'if by any chance it *does* go, then I agree with you – you'll be certain to miss it now. Why don't you resign yourself to that?'

She turned away and peered through the windows at the fog. It seemed to be getting thicker as they went along, and now she could only just make out the edge of the road and the margin of grassland beyond it. She knew that her husband was still looking at her. She glanced at him again, and this time she noticed with a kind of horror that he was staring intently at the little place in the corner of her left eye where she could feel the muscle twitching.

'Won't you?' he said.

'Won't I what?'

'Be sure to miss it now if it goes. We can't drive fast in this muck.'*

He didn't speak to her any more after that. The car crawled on and on. The driver had a yellow lamp directed on to the edge of the road, and this helped him to keep going. Other lights, some white and some yellow, kept coming out of the fog towards them, and there was an especially bright one that followed close behind them all the time.

Suddenly, the driver stopped the car.

'There!' Mr Foster cried. 'We're stuck. I knew it.'

'No, sir,' the driver said, turning round. 'We made it. This is the airport.'

Without a word, Mrs Foster jumped out and hurried through the main entrance into the building. There was a mass of people inside, mostly disconsolate passengers standing around the ticket counters. She pushed her way through and spoke to the clerk.

'Yes,' he said. 'Your flight is temporarily postponed. But please don't go away. We're expecting this weather to clear any moment.'

She went back to her husband who was still sitting in the car and told him the news. 'But don't you wait, dear,' she said. 'There's no sense in that.'

'I won't,' he answered. 'So long as the driver can get me back. Can you get me back, driver?'

'I think so,' the man said.

'Is the luggage out?'

'Yes, sir.'

'Good-bye, dear,' Mrs Foster said, leaning into the car and giving her husband a small kiss on the coarse grey fur of his cheek.

'Good-bye,' he answered. 'Have a good trip.'

The car drove off, and Mrs Foster was left alone.

The rest of the day was a sort of nightmare for her. She sat for hour after hour on a bench, as close to the airline counter as possible, and every thirty minutes or so she would get up and ask the clerk if the situation had changed. She always received the same reply – that she must continue to wait, because the fog might blow away at any moment. It wasn't until after six in the evening that the loudspeakers finally announced that the flight had been postponed until eleven o'clock the next morning.

Mrs Foster didn't quite know what to do when she heard this news. She stayed sitting on her bench for at least another half-hour, wondering, in a tired, hazy sort of way, where she might go to spend the night. She hated to leave the airport. She didn't wish to see her husband. She was terrified that in one way or another he would eventually manage to prevent her from getting to France. She would have liked to remain just where she was, sitting on the bench the whole night through. That would be the safest. But she was already exhausted, and it didn't take her long to realize that this was a ridiculous thing for an elderly lady to do. So in the end she went to a phone and called the house.

Her husband, who was on the point of leaving for the club, answered it himself. She told him the news, and asked whether the servants were still there.

'They've all gone,' he said.

'In that case, dear, I'll just get myself a room somewhere for the night. And don't you bother yourself about it at all.'

'That would be foolish,' he said. 'You've got a large house here at your disposal. Use it.'

'But, dear, it's *empty*.'

'Then I'll stay with you myself.'

'There's no food in the house. There's nothing.'

'Then eat before you come in. Don't be so stupid, woman. Everything you do, you seem to want to make a fuss about it.'

'Yes,' she said. 'I'm sorry. I'll get myself a sandwich here, and then I'll come on in.'

Outside, the fog had cleared a little, but it was still a long, slow drive in the taxi, and she didn't arrive back at the house on Sixty-second Street until fairly late.

Her husband emerged from his study when he heard her coming in. 'Well,' he said, standing by the study door, 'how was Paris?'

'We leave at eleven in the morning,' she answered. 'It's definite.'

'You mean if the fog clears.'

'It's clearing now. There's a wind coming up.'

'You look tired,' he said. 'You must have had an anxious day.'

'It wasn't very comfortable. I think I'll go straight to bed.'

'I've ordered a car for the morning,' he said. 'Nine o'clock.'

'Oh, thank you, dear. And I certainly hope you're not going to bother to come all the way out again to see me off.'

'No,' he said slowly. 'I don't think I will. But there's no reason why you shouldn't drop me at the club on your way.'

She looked at him, and at that moment he seemed to be standing a long way off from her, beyond some borderline. He was suddenly so small and far away that she couldn't be sure what he was doing, or what he was thinking, or even what he was.

'The club is downtown,' she said. 'It isn't on the way to the airport.'

'But you'll have plenty of time, my dear. Don't you want to drop me at the club?'

'Oh, yes – of course.'

'That's good. Then I'll see you in the morning at nine.'

She went up to her bedroom on the second floor, and she was so exhausted from her day that she fell asleep soon after she lay down.

Next morning, Mrs Foster was up early, and by eight-thirty she was downstairs and ready to leave.

37

Roald Dahl

Shortly after nine, her husband appeared. 'Did you make any coffee?' he asked.

'No, dear. I thought you'd get a nice breakfast at the club. The car is here. It's been waiting. I'm all ready to go.'

They were standing in the hall – they always seemed to be meeting in the hall nowadays – she with her hat and coat and purse, he in a curiously cut Edwardian* jacket with high lapels.

'Your luggage?'

'It's at the airport.'

'Ah yes,' he said. 'Of course. And if you're going to take me to the club first, I suppose we'd better get going fairly soon, hadn't we?'

'Yes!' she cried. 'Oh, yes – *please!*'

'I'm just going to get a few cigars. I'll be right with you. You get in the car.'

She turned and went out to where the chauffeur was standing, and he opened the car door for her as she approached.

'What time is it?' she asked him.

'About nine-fifteen.'

Mr Foster came out five minutes later, and watching him as he walked slowly down the steps, she noticed that his legs were like a goat's legs in those narrow stovepipe trousers that he wore. As on the day before, he paused half-way down to sniff the air and to examine the sky. The weather was still not quite clear, but there was a wisp of sun coming through the mist.

'Perhaps you'll be lucky this time,' he said as he settled himself beside her in the car.

'Hurry, please,' she said to the chauffeur. 'Don't bother about the rug. I'll arrange the rug. Please get going. I'm late.'

The man went back to his seat behind the wheel and started the engine.

'*Just* a moment!' Mr Foster said suddenly. 'Hold it a moment, chauffeur, will you?'

'What is it, dear?' She saw him searching the pockets of his overcoat.

'I had a little present I wanted you to take to Ellen,' he said. 'Now, where on earth is it? I'm sure I had it in my hand as I came down.'

'I never saw you carrying anything. What sort of present?'

'A little box wrapped up in white paper. I forgot to give it to you yesterday. I don't want to forget it today.'

'A little box!' Mrs Foster cried. 'I never saw any little box!' She began hunting frantically in the back of the car.

Her husband continued searching through the pockets of his coat. Then he unbuttoned the coat and felt around in his jacket. 'Confound it,' he said, 'I must've left it in my bedroom. I won't be a moment.'

'Oh, *please*!' she cried. 'We haven't got time! *Please* leave it! You can mail it. It's only one of those silly combs anyway. You're always giving her combs.'

'And what's wrong with combs, may I ask?' he said, furious that she should have forgotten herself for once.

'Nothing, dear, I'm sure. But . . .'

'Stay here!' he commanded. 'I'm going to get it.'

'Be quick, dear! Oh, *please* be quick!'

She sat still, waiting and waiting.

'Chauffeur, what time is it?'

The man had a wristwatch, which he consulted. 'I make it nearly nine-thirty.'

'Can we get to the airport in an hour?'

'Just about.'

At this point, Mrs Foster suddenly spotted a corner of something white wedged down in the crack of the seat on the side where her husband had been sitting. She reached over and pulled out a small paper-wrapped box, and at the same time she couldn't help noticing that it was wedged down firm and deep, as though with the help of a pushing hand.

'Here it is!' she cried. 'I've found it! Oh dear, and now he'll be up there for ever searching for it! Chauffeur, quickly – run in and call him down, will you please?'

The chauffeur, a man with a small rebellious Irish mouth, didn't care very much for any of this, but he climbed out of the car and went up the steps to the front door of the house. Then he turned and came back. 'Door's locked,' he announced. 'You got a key?'

'Yes – wait a minute.' She began hunting madly in her purse. The little face was screwed up tight with anxiety, the lips pushed outward like a spout.

'Here it is! No – I'll go myself. It'll be quicker. I know where he'll be.'

She hurried out of the car and up the steps to the front door, holding the key in one hand. She slid the key into the keyhole and was about to turn it – and then she stopped. Her head came up, and she stood there absolutely motionless, her whole body arrested right in the middle of all this hurry to turn the key and get into the house, and she waited – five, six, seven, eight, nine, ten seconds, she waited. The way she was standing there, with her head in the air and the body so tense, it seemed as though she were listening for the repetition of some sound that she had heard a moment before from a place far away inside the house.

Yes – quite obviously she was listening. Her whole attitude was a *listening* one. She appeared actually to be moving one of her ears closer and closer to the door. Now it was right up against the door, and for still another few seconds she remained in that position, head up, ear to door, hand on key, about to enter but not entering, trying instead, or so it seemed, to hear and to analyse these sounds that were coming faintly from this place deep within the house.

Then, all at once, she sprang to life again. She withdrew the key from the door and came running back down the steps.

'It's too late!' she cried to the chauffeur. 'I can't wait for him, I simply can't. I'll miss the plane. Hurry now, driver, hurry! To the airport!'

The chauffeur, had he been watching her closely, might have noticed that her face had turned absolutely white and that the whole expression had suddenly altered. There was no longer that rather soft and silly look. A peculiar hardness had settled itself upon the features. The little mouth, usually so flabby, was now tight and thin, the eyes were bright, and the voice, when she spoke, carried a new note of authority.

'Hurry, driver, hurry!'

'Isn't your husband travelling with you?' the man asked, astonished.

'Certainly not! I was only going to drop him at the club. It won't matter. He'll understand. He'll get a cab.* Don't sit there talking, man. *Get going*! I've got a plane to catch for Paris!'

With Mrs Foster urging him from the back seat, the man drove fast all the way, and she caught her plane with a few minutes to spare. Soon she was high up over the Atlantic, reclining comfortably in her aeroplane chair, listening to the hum of the motors, heading for Paris at last. The new mood was still with her. She felt remarkably strong and, in a queer sort of way, wonderful. She was a trifle breathless with it all, but this was more from pure astonishment at what she had done than anything else, and as the plane flew farther and farther away from New York and East Sixty-second Street, a great sense of calmness began to settle upon her. By the

41

time she reached Paris, she was just as strong and cool and calm as she could wish.

She met her grandchildren, and they were even more beautiful in the flesh than in their photographs. They were like angels, she told herself, so beautiful they were. And every day she took them for walks, and fed them cakes, and bought them presents, and told them charming stories.

Once a week, on Tuesdays, she wrote a letter to her husband – a nice, chatty letter – full of news and gossip, which always ended with the words 'Now be sure to take your meals regularly, dear, although this is something I'm afraid you may not be doing when I'm not with you.'

When the six weeks were up, everybody was sad that she had to return to America, to her husband. Everybody, that is, except her. Surprisingly, she didn't seem to mind as much as one might have expected, and when she kissed them all good-bye, there was something in her manner and in the things she said that appeared to hint at the possibility of a return in the not too distant future.

However, like the faithful wife she was, she did not overstay her time. Exactly six weeks after she had arrived, she sent a cable* to her husband and caught the plane back to New York.

Arriving at Idlewild, Mrs Foster was interested to observe that there was no car to meet her. It is possible that she might even have been a little amused. But she was extremely calm and did not overtip* the porter who helped her into a taxi with her baggage.

New York was colder than Paris, and there were lumps of dirty snow lying in the gutters of the streets. The taxi drew up before the house on Sixty-second Street, and Mrs Foster persuaded the driver to carry her two large cases to the top of the steps. Then she paid him off and rang the bell. She waited, but there was no answer. Just to make sure, she rang again, and she could hear it tinkling shrilly far away in the pantry, at the back of the house. But still no one came.

So she took out her own key and opened the door herself.

The first thing she saw as she entered was a great pile of mail lying on the floor where it had fallen after being slipped through the letter box. The place was dark and cold. A dust sheet was still draped over the grandfather clock. In spite of the cold, the atmosphere was peculiarly oppressive, and there was a faint and curious odour in the air that she had never smelled before.

She walked quickly across the hall and disappeared for a moment around the corner to the left, at the back. There was something deliberate and purposeful about this action; she had the air of a woman who is off to investigate a rumour or to confirm a suspicion. And when she returned a few seconds later, there was a little glimmer of satisfaction on her face.

She paused in the centre of the hall, as though wondering what to do next. Then, suddenly, she turned and went across into her husband's study. On the desk she found his address book, and after hunting through it for a while she picked up the phone and dialled a number.

'Hello,' she said. 'Listen – this is Nine East Sixty-second Street . . . Yes, that's right. Could you send someone round as soon as possible, do you think? Yes, it seems to be stuck between the second and third floors. At least, that's where the indicator's pointing . . . Right away? Oh, that's very kind of you. You see, my legs aren't any too good for walking up a lot of stairs. Thank you so much. Good-bye.'

She replaced the receiver and sat there at her husband's desk, patiently waiting for the man who would be coming soon to repair the lift.

Glossary

page 28
theatre curtain: the start of a play when the curtain goes up

page 29
foible: peculiar mannerism

page 30
Idlewild: New York's main airport, now called J. F. Kennedy
  airport

page 32
dapper: of neat, smart appearance
Andrew Carnegie: American industrialist and philanthropist
  (1835–1919)
the Park: Central Park in the heart of New York City

page 33
club: the place where the members (here all male) of a social
  organization can stay
hold with: agree with, approve of

page 34
muck: thick fog

page 38
Edwardian: typical of the period just before the First World
  War (King Edward VII reigned 1901–10)

page 41
cab: taxi

page 42
cable: telegram
overtip: give more money than necessary for the porter's
  service

44

Questions

1 What evidence is there in the story that the Fosters are wealthy?
2 What is Mr Foster's attitude to his servants?
3 Describe the character of Mrs Foster as accurately as possible. How likeable do you find her?
4 In what ways does Mrs Foster's attitude towards her husband change during the story?
5 How do you think the small white box had become wedged down the side of the back seat of the car?
6 When Mrs Foster arrived back in New York and found there was no car to meet her at the airport we are told, 'It is possible that she might even have been a little amused' (page 42). Why was this?
7 What in fact had happened to Mr Foster while his wife was in Paris?

Topics for discussion

1 'It was really extraordinary how in certain people a simple apprehension about a thing like catching a train can grow into a serious obsession' (page 28) Do you have any similar obsessions? How do you try to deal with them?
2 What is your opinion of Mr Foster's reaction to his wife's obsession?
3 How would you have reacted?
4 Is the author's sympathy more with Mrs Foster or her husband? Give reasons for your answer.
5 What do you think made Mrs Foster suddenly decide to leave for the airport alone on the second morning?
6 Why do you think Mrs Foster was quite pleased to return to New York?
7 Did you expect the story to end the way it does? If not, how did you think it would end?
8 Did you enjoy the story? Why (not)?

H. E. Bates
Time

H. E. Bates was born in England in 1905 and worked as a
journalist before publishing his first book The Two
Sisters in 1925. Before the Second World War he wrote
several short stories about the English countryside.
Perhaps his most famous stories, including Fair Stood
the Wind for France (1944), were written by him as
'Flying Officer X' during the war. After the war he
wrote two very successful novels set in Burma, The
Purple Plain (1947) and The Jacaranda Tree (1949).
More recently he has concentrated on novels set in
England, like The Darling Buds of May (1958) and Oh!
To be in England (1963).

   'Time' is an amusing story of two senile old men
whose lives are brightened up by their youthful-seeming
companion Duke, who isn't as honest or quite as
marvellous as they believe.

Sitting on an iron seat fixed about the body of a great
chestnut tree breaking into pink-flushed blossom, two
old men gazed dumbly at the sunlit emptiness of a town
square.

   The morning sun burned in a sky of marvellous blue
serenity, making the drooping leaves of the tree most
brilliant and the pale blossoms expand to fullest beauty.
The eyes of the old men were also blue, but the brilliance of the summer sky made a mockery of the dim
and somnolent light in them. Their thin white hair and

drooping skin, their faltering lips and rusted clothes, the huddling bones of their bodies had come to winter.* Their hands tottered,* their lips were wet and dribbling, and they stared with a kind of earnest vacancy, seeing the world as a stillness of amber mist. They were perpetually silent, for the deafness of one made speech a ghastly effort of shouting and misinterpretation. With their worn sticks between their knees and their worn hands knotted over their sticks they sat as though time had ceased to exist for them.

Nevertheless every movement across the square was an event. Their eyes missed nothing that came within sight. It was as if the passing of every vehicle held for them the possibility of catastrophe; the appearance of a strange face was a revolution; the apparitions of young ladies in light summer dresses gliding on legs of shell-pink silk had on them something of the effect of goddesses on the minds of young heroes. There were, sometimes, subtle changes of light in their eyes.

Across the square, they observed an approaching figure. They watched it with a new intensity, exchanging also, for the first time, a glance with one another. For the first time also they spoke.

'Who is it?' said one.

'Duke, ain't* it?'

'Looks like Duke,' the other said. 'But I can't see that far.'

Leaning forward on their sticks, they watched the approach of this figure with intent expectancy. He, too, was old. Beside him, indeed, it was as if they were adolescent. He was patriarchal. He resembled a Biblical prophet, bearded and white and immemorial. He was timeless.

But though he looked like a patriarch he came across the square with the haste of a man in a walking race. He moved with a nimbleness and airiness* that were miraculous. Seeing the old men on the seat he waved his stick with an amazing gaiety at them. It was like the brandishing of a youthful sword. Ten yards away he bellowed their names lustily in greeting.

'Well, Reuben boy! Well, Shepherd!'

They mumbled sombrely in reply. He shouted stentoriously* about the weather, wagging his white beard strongly. They shifted stiffly along the seat and he sat down. A look of secret relief came over their dim faces, for he had towered above them like a statue in silver and bronze.

'Thought maybe you warn't* coming,' mumbled Reuben.

'Ah! been for a sharp* walk!' he half-shouted. 'A sharp walk.'

They had not the courage to ask where he had walked, but in his clear brisk voice he told them, and deducing that he could not have travelled less than six or seven miles they sat in gloomy silence, as though shamed. With relief they saw him fumble in his pockets and bring out a bag of peppermints, black-and-white balls sticky and strong from the heat of his strenuous body, and having one by one popped peppermints into their mouths they sucked for a long time with toothless and dumb solemnity, contemplating the sunshine.

As they sucked, the two old men waited for Duke to speak, and they waited like men awaiting an oracle, since he was, in their eyes, a masterpiece of a man. Long ago, when they had been napkinned and at the breast, he had been a man with a beard, and before they had reached their youth he had passed into a lusty maturity. All their lives they had felt infantile beside him.

Now, in old age, he persisted in shaming them by the lustiness of his achievements and his vitality. He had the secret of devilish perpetual youth. To them the world across the square was veiled in sunny mistiness, but

Duke could detect the swiftness of a rabbit on a hill-side a mile away. They heard the sounds of the world as though through a stone wall, but he could hear the crisp bark of a fox in another parish. They were condemned to an existence of memory because they could not read, but Duke devoured* the papers. He had an infinite knowledge of the world and the freshest* affairs of men. He brought them, every morning, news of earthquakes in Peru, of wars in China, of assassinations in Spain of scandals among the clergy.* He understood the obscurest movements of politicians and explained to them the newest laws of the land. They listened to him with the devoutness of worshippers listening to a preacher, regarding him with awe and believing in him with humble astonishment. There were times when he lied to them blatantly.* They never suspected.

As they sat there, blissfully sucking, the shadow of the chestnut tree began to shorten, its westward edge creeping up, like a tide, towards their feet. Beyond, the sun continued to blaze with unbroken brilliance on the white square. Swallowing the last smooth grain of peppermint, Reuben wondered aloud what time it could be.

'Time?' said Duke. He spoke ominously. 'Time?' he repeated.

They watched his hand solemnly uplift itself and vanish into his breast. They had no watches. Duke alone could tell them the passage of time while appearing to mock at it himself. Very slowly he drew out an immense watch, held it out at length on its silver chain, and regarded it steadfastly.

They regarded it also, at first with humble solemnity and then with quiet astonishment. They leaned forward to stare at it. Their eyes were filled with a great light of unbelief. The watch had stopped.

The three old men continued to stare at the watch in

silence. The stopping of this watch was like the stopping of some perfect automaton. It resembled almost the stopping of time itself. Duke shook the watch urgently. The hands moved onwards for a second or two from half-past three and then were dead again. He lifted it to his ear and listened. It was silent.

For a moment or two longer the old man sat in lug-ubrious* contemplation. The watch, like Duke, was a masterpiece, incredibly ancient, older even than Duke himself. They did not know how often he had boasted to them of its age and efficiency, its beauty and price-lessness.* They remembered that it had once belonged to his father, that he had been offered incredible sums for it, that it had never stopped since the battle of Waterloo.*

Finally Duke spoke. He spoke with the mysterious air of a man about to unravel a mystery, 'Know what 'tis?'

They could only shake their heads and stare with the blankness of ignorance and curiosity. They could not know.

Duke made an ominous gesture, almost a flourish, with the hand that held the watch.

'It's the lectric.'*

They stared at him with dim-eyed amazement.

'It's the lectric,' he repeated. 'The lectric in me* body.'

Shepherd was deaf. 'Eh?' he said.

'The lectric,' said Duke significantly, in a louder voice.

'Lectric?' They did not understand, and they waited.

The oracle spoke at last, repeating with one hand the ominous gesture that was like a flourish.

'It stopped yesterday. Stopped in the middle of me dinner,' he said. He was briefly silent. 'Never stopped as long as I can remember. Never. And then stopped like that, all of a sudden, just at pudden-time.* Couldn't understand it. Couldn't understand it for the life of me.'

'Take it to the watchmaker's?' Reuben said.

'I did,' he said. 'I did. This watch is older'n me, I said, and it's never stopped as long as I can remember. So he squinted at it and poked it and that's what he said.'

'What?'

'It's the lectric, he says, that's what it is. It's the lectric – the lectric in your body. That's what he said. The lectric.'

'Lectric light?'

'That's what he said. Lectric. You're full o' lectric, he says. You go home and leave your watch on the the shelf and it'll go again. So I did.'

The eyes of the old men seemed to signal intense questions. There was an ominous silence. Finally, with the watch still in his hand, Duke made an immense flourish, a gesture of serene triumph.

'And it went,' he said. 'It went!'

The old men murmured in wonder.

'It went all right. Right as a cricket!* Beautiful!'

The eyes of the old men flickered with fresh amazement. The fickleness* of the watch was beyond the weakness of their ancient comprehension. They groped for understanding as they might have searched with their dim eyes for a balloon far up in the sky. Staring and murmuring they could only pretend to understand.

'Solid truth,' said Duke. 'Goes on the shelf but it won't go on me. It's the lectric.'

'That's what licks* me,' said Reuben, 'the lectric.'

'It's me body,' urged Duke. 'It's full of it.'

'Lectric light?'

'Full of it. Alive with it.'

He spoke like a man who had won a prize. Bursting with glory, he feigned humility. His white beard wagged lustily with pride, but the hand still bearing the watch seemed to droop with modesty.

'It's the lectric,' he boasted softly.

They accepted the words in silence. It was as though they began to understand at last the lustiness of Duke's life, the nimbleness of his mind, the amazing youthfulness of his patriarchal limbs.

The shadow of the chestnut tree had dwindled to a small dark circle about their seat. The rays of the sun were brilliantly perpendicular. On the chestnut tree itself the countless candelabra of blossoms were a pure blaze of white and rose. A clock began to chime for noon.*

Duke, at that moment, looked at his watch, still lying in his hand.

He stared with instant guilt. The hands had moved miraculously to four o'clock, and in the stillness of the summer air he could hear the tick of wheels.

With hasty gesture of resignation he dropped the watch into his pocket again. He looked quickly at the old men, but they were sunk in sombre meditation. They had not seen or heard.

Abruptly he rose. 'That's what it is,' he said. 'The lectric.' He made a last gesture as though to indicate that he was the victim of some divine manifestation. 'The lectric,' he said.

He retreated nimbly across the square in the hot sunshine and the older men sat staring after him with the innocence of solemn wonder. His limbs moved with the haste of a clockwork doll, and he vanished with incredible swiftness from sight.

The sun had crept beyond the zenith* and the feet of the old men were bathed in sunshine.

Glossary

page 47
winter: the last stage of their lives; like the last season of the year.
tottered: shook unsteadily
ain't it (= isn't it)
airiness: lightness of movement

page 48
stentoriously: very loudly
warn't (= weren't)
sharp: quick

page 49
devoured: read with eager interest
freshest: latest, most up to date
the clergy: priests of the church
blatantly: very obviously and deliberately

page 50
lugubrious: sad, gloomy
pricelessness: so valuable that one cannot estimate its real value
battle of Waterloo: the battle fought near Brussels in which Napoleon was defeated by the Anglo-Prussian alliance in 1815
lectric (= electricity)
me (= my)
pudden-time: (= pudding time) when he was eating his dessert

page 51
right as a cricket!: in perfect condition
fickleness: unreliability
licks: (slang) defeats, is incomprehensible

page 52
noon: mid-day
zenith: highest point

Questions

1 What was the day like on which this story took place?
2 Describe some of the differences between Duke on the one hand, and Reuben and Shepherd on the other.
3 Give some reasons why, in the eyes of Reuben and Shepherd, Duke seemed to be 'a masterpiece of a man' (page 48).
4 How far in reality do you think their belief is justified?
5 What importance does Duke's watch have in the context of the whole story?
6 What do the two old men accept is the key to Duke's apparent eternal youthfulness?
7 What evidence is there that Duke is dishonest?
8 Why does Duke leave his two companions so suddenly?

Topics for discussion

1 Do you find Duke a likeable character? Give reasons for your answer.
2 Do you think the story mainly depends upon the plot, the characters or the setting?
3 What different aspects of time do you think are suggested in the story?
4 When you are old, would you prefer to be like Duke or the other two old men?
5 Describe an old man you have known personally and particularly liked.
6 What do you think makes the ending of a short story successful? How far does the end of this story fulfil your requirements?
7 In what ways did you enjoy the story (or not)?

Morris Lurie
A King of the Road

Morris Lurie, who was born in Melbourne in 1938,
studied architecture, has worked in advertising, and is
now one of a group of well-known young Australian
writers. Lurie spent much of the 1960s and early 70s
living in London, and it was there that his first collection
of short stories Happy Times *was published in 1969, and*
most recently, Running Nicely, *in 1979. His work has*
regularly appeared in prominent British and American
literary magazines. He has also written novels including
Rappaport *(1966),* The Jungle Adventures of Charlie
Hope *(1968) and* Rappaport's Revenge *(1972).*
    'A King of the Road' is an amusing story, seen from
the point of view of a young Jewish boy, about his
father's adventures in first refusing to buy, then buying a
car.

You can lead a horse to water, but you can't make my
father buy a car. Master psychologists have tried. For
example, my mother. 'Abe, let's buy a car,' she says. 'I
don't need it,' my father says. 'What for?' And he takes
down our perfectly all right toaster* from its shelf and
gets busy on it with the small screwdriver which he
always carries, and at such moments, when he's fixing*
no one talks to him.

    We move forward a month. Picture a spring night, a
star-crammed sky, a black Pontiac stopping at our front
gate. My father gets out first, then my mother. My

mother tells Uncle Sam for the twentieth time to thank Tzila for the wonderful supper, really, she shouldn't have gone to all that trouble, and then, catching up with my father who already has his key in the front door lock, she says, 'See how it is when you have a car? Right to the door.' 'A nice lift,'* my father says.

How long does the water-on-stone treatment* take? I lie in my bed and listen to it happening, drip, drip, at the other end of the passage, in my parents' bed. A month, two? Time doesn't mean anything. Occasionally I hear a loud No!' and from its violence I know that things are about to happen.

And they do. One Sunday morning, when I have stew-ed* in my bed past the point of pleasure, I get up and my father is not at home. 'Where's Dad?' I ask my mother. For every Sunday for as long as I can remember, my father has been out in the garden, either mowing a lawn or pulling up weeds or just standing and thinking about one of those two. 'Don't bother me, can't you see I'm busy,' my mother says. She has taken out all the cutlery and is lining the drawers with new white paper, a thing which she does only for *pesach*,* or if someone spills something in a drawer, but never at any other time. No answer. I make a breakfast. An hour later my father comes in, looking flushed.* 'Well?' my mother asks. 'I don't need a car!' my father says. 'What for?' The driving lessons have begun.

The next Sunday I am awake at seven, dressed in five minutes, sitting on my bed and then standing up and then sitting down again, a thousand times, waiting for my father to go out and begin his lessons. I hear a car toot.* My father is in the kitchen drinking tea, and I hear the cup fall from his hands, with an enormous sound, as though every piece of china in our kitchen has been broken, and then I hear him moving quickly down the passage, fumbling with the front door, the door slamming, and then my father's steps running down the path. I am also out, also running, but quietly, and from the front room window, concealed behind the drawn blind, I see everything.

There is a short, bald man sitting at the wheel of a large green car. He sees my father. He slides over on the seat, leans over and opens the door, and my father gets in. They talk for a long time, the man pointing, my father nodding. Then the car starts. My father's face is a study of concentration and terror. He looks at the bald man. The man points to something. My father does something with his hands, then puts them both on the wheel, high up, and I see, or feel, how white his knuckles are. Then the car begins to move.

It shoots forward, stops, bounces, seems to come back, then forward again, up into the air, over to one side, and I hide my face. And when next I look, the street in front of our house is empty.

I run outside, forgetting all caution, all stealth!* And I am just in time. The green car is at the very end of our street, where it meets the main road, and it's not moving. I watch it, and it seems to stand there for ever, hours, while my heart waits too. Then suddenly it is gone, as though wires have jerked it round the corner, and I breathe out.

I don't bother to wait around to see my father drive back. Everyone has difficulties at the beginning, I rationalize; it's only natural, after all. But something has died inside me. When he comes back from his lesson I am mowing the lawn and frightened to look him in the eye. I mow like a madman, front *and* back, and then I start on the weeds, and the only thing that stops me finishing them is my mother calling me in to lunch. Never again do I go out to see the lesson begin, not once.

Once again time has no meaning. Months pass, one after another, and it is as though my father has always

gone for driving lessons on a Sunday morning; I can't
remember a time when he didn't. And when my Uncle
Sam drops around* and says to my father, 'So, you're
taking the lessons, uh?' and slaps my father on the
shoulder, I leave the room.

Naturally, it's me who brings in the letter with the
picture-window envelope and my father's name typed
inside. 'Ah,' says my father, getting his toaster-fixing
hands to it as though it was the last *latke** in the world,
while I feign* indifference. But at the dinner table I am
spared nothing. The talk is all of licences, only licences,
and this licence, my father's, is held up and waved and
shown and finally my father lets it out of his hand for
just a few seconds and lets me hold it. 'Nu, scholar,' he
says, 'can you read it?' and snatches it away before I
have even had a chance to focus. 'You know how long it
took Max Lazarus to get this, this piece of paper? Nu?
Ten months! Ha! And about his wife I'm not even
going to mention.' While my mother, the master
psychologist, serves the soup and says not a word.

Now the talking in bed starts again, the soft voices in
the dark, the whispers, and then the loud 'No!' while I
lie in my bed and strain for details. But this time there is
no secrecy.

My father announces, the next night, that he is
going to buy a car, he has decided, even the colour he
knows. Blue, in two shades, the lighter one on the top,
like the Finkelsteins have. Well, not exactly like the Finkelsteins have, theirs is the old model, already out of
date. 'Tomorrow I put down my name,' he says, looking
already a good three feet taller than he actually is.
'Eight months,' he says to me. 'For such a car, you have
to wait eight months. Don't worry, I'll get it in six.'

Once again I lose track of the time, but as the months
creep past, and speed, and lunge forward, and relent-
lessly advance, I keep surprising my father, sitting all

alone in the front room with the light off, his licence held in both hands, his eyes riveted* to it. 'Oh, I'm sorry,' I say, having switched on the light, 'I didn't know you were ... I wanted to hear something on the radio.' 'I don't want the radio!' my father shouts, and stands up and lunges out of the room, putting the licence away quickly inside his wallet, pushing the wallet down deep inside his trouser pocket, then standing in the passage, not knowing where to go.

This happens again and again, maybe four times. As the time for the car's arrival draws near, my father grows more and more quiet. To speak to him is at your own risk. Even my mother, that master psychologist, can't draw near. 'Abe, maybe you should have a few more lessons, to brush up,'* she says. 'You know, to get the feel.' 'No!' my father shouts, and it is only his iron will that keeps him from taking out his licence at the table and staring at it.

Then one night, a Thursday, the phone rings. My mother answers. I hear her talking for a half minute, and then she says, 'Just a minute, I'll get him,' and then she calls out, 'Abe, for you! The car!'

My father scrambles to his feet and his face is flushed and ashen* at the same time. He holds the telephone receiver as I saw him holding the wheel of the green car for his second lesson. 'Hello?' he says, in a voice I have never heard him use before. 'Tomorrow? All right. I'll, yes ...' and the phone falls from his fingers.

'Tomorrow,' he says to my mother, who is standing a foot away, about six inches from me.

'Well, ring up Sam and tell him to go with you,' my mother says.

'I don't need Sam,' my father says. 'I can drive.'

'The city traffic, Abe,' my mother says, and my father says, 'You call him.'

My mother dials, and gets, of course, Aunt Tzila, who

59

is always first to the phone. 'Tzila?' she says, 'the car has arrived. What? Yes, we just heard, now, on the telephone, they rang us up, it's ready.' 'Nu?' says my father, suddenly impatient. 'C'mon,* let me speak.' And he takes the receiver out of my mother's hand while she is in the middle of a word, explaining that it is a two shades of blue car, like the Finkelsteins, but, naturally, a new model . . .

'Tzila?' my father says. 'Thank you, thank you. Naah,* I'm not excited, what's a car? It's a machine, that's all. Yes, a blue, two shades, that's what I ordered. Blue is a good colour, you don't have to wash it so much. Ha ha, yeah . . . Listen, is Sam there?'

There is a pause for some seconds while Aunt Tzila calls out to Sam that he's wanted on the phone, it's the car, it's arrived, a blue one, two shades.

'Hello, Sam?' my father says. 'Listen . . . yeah, tomorrow. Listen, Sam, maybe it would be a good idea if . . . ah! There? In the showroom? Four o'clock. Come a bit earlier, so we can . . . Four o'clock? Nu, good. What? Just a minute, I'll put her back on, she's standing right here. Four o'clock, all right?'

And he gives the phone back to my mother, so she can speak some more with Aunt Tzila, and then, unable to employ his iron will a second longer, he plunges his hand into his pocket, draws out the wallet, with loving care unfolds the licence from its place inside, and studies it, really studies it, until he looks up and sees me watching him. 'You haven't got any lessons?' he shouts at me, and I flee to the sanity of my room.

Four o'clock the following afternoon I am already standing outside our house, waiting. And so is everyone else in our street. Somehow the word has spread. All the street is in their gardens or standing and talking, looking nonchalant,* but I know what they're waiting to see. Even Mr Pinter, who hasn't spoken to my father in four years, after some difference of opinion which time has long obliterated, is there.

Only my mother won't come outside. 'I'll come, I'll come,' she says to me, but she stays inside.

It is half past four. The street is still empty of the car. Now, if anything, there are more people than ever, and their nonchalance has gone. For all their talking and occasionally laughing, I can feel an electric tension in the street. In just a few minutes, a second, one beat of my heart . . .

And then the car appears.

We see it turning slowly into the street, two shades of blue, my father at the wheel. It makes an elaborate turn, and then pauses, and begins again. The street is quiet.

'Mum!' I call out, but she is already there, by my side.

'*He's* driving,' my mother says. 'Why isn't Sam driving?'

But it is my father at the wheel. Sam is sitting next to him, a separate shape.

'Mum, don't worry,' I say, or shout, or something, running out into the street, then back onto the nature strip, and then out into the street again.

The car comes closer. It is moving as quietly as a stream of oil, as slowly as a dream. Now it is close enough for me to see my father's face. It is like a tomato, the sun, beaming, shining, bursting, and his smile is enormous. I have never seen my father look so radiant, like a king on the field of battle when the enemy has fled.

My father smiles to everyone, on both sides of the street, as he drives his brand-new* car. He smiles to Mr Pinter, who shrinks, to the two ladies at number twelve, to the Obers, the Winters, to all. And then I see Uncle Sam lean over and say something to him and point at something inside the car and my father looks down for a second and does something with his hand and then looks up again, his face serious now for a second, though still bright red, and then the smile comes back, and now he is almost at our house and beginning to turn – our gates are open, the garage yawns wide – and his smile is still enormous and in this fashion my father drives into our fence.

'Oh!' gasps my mother, inside her throat.

The car shakes, shudders, stops. A door flies open. My Uncle Sam is out. 'Nothing, nothing,' he says, and he is running to the front of the car, bending to see what has happened, looking up at my mother, then back to the front of the car, then at my father, who hasn't moved. He sits, his hands still on the wheel, the colour draining out of him like a stone.

'My God!' says my mother, a hand to her heart.

'Don't worry, don't worry,' Uncle Sam says, and he runs around behind the car and comes up and opens the door on my father's side.

'I'll fix it,' he says. Like a stone, my father gets out.

Now, expertly, in a flurry of gears, looking at no one and at everyone, craning his neck to see behind him, sitting up straight, moving like a machine, he shoots the car back, corrects its angle, and whips it up* our drive and into the garage.

I run to see what has happened. My mother is a step behind me. My father stands on the nature strip, not moving.

Uncle Sam is out of the car, the keys in his hand. He has a kind of smile on his face. 'Ah, it's . . .' he starts to say, but we push past him and rush to the front of the car and stare at it.

There is a dent in the front bumper* about the size of a pea.

'My God!' says my mother, again and again, over and over, shaking from side to side, as the old Mrs Fisher does on Yom Kippur,* totally immersed in her prayers.

Uncle Sam stands with the keys in his hand and doesn't know what to do. He begins to say something, 'Ah, believe me, *my* first car, you should have seen how . . .'

He stops. No one is listening to him. My father has come up the drive and is standing next to him, looking at the car but not going around to see the front of it.

'The fence is all right,' he says.

Finally my mother is persuaded to come inside, what's the point of standing here? 'I'll have a cup of tea,' Uncle Sam says, smacking his hands together, smiling, but no one is fooled.* I am sent to close the front gates.

My mother makes the tea and Uncle Sam tells us all, at least three times, how it was with his first car, why, this is nothing, not even an accident. And my father drinks his tea and doesn't say a word. Nor does my mother. Both my parents are deep inside themselves.

When Uncle Sam has gone – 'Don't worry, Abe,' patting my father on the arm – my mother suddenly comes alive. 'Go in your room. It's enough for one day,' she says to me, and she closes the kitchen door and – but I'm not sure about this – locks it.

Then I hear their voices, now loud, now soft, and then my mother opens the door and goes to the telephone, closing another door so I can't hear what she's saying, and then when she has finished there she calls me to come out.

We eat in total silence, not a word. When we are drinking our tea, my father says, 'I'm selling the car,' and then picks up his cup and ends the matter with a loud sip of his tea.

The next morning, before eight, two men come and take away the car. I watch them signing papers, and then they hand my father a cheque, and he puts it inside his wallet and shakes their hands and goes out with

63

them to the garage, but that part I don't watch. Who wants to see a brand-new car, two shades of blue, being driven away at eight o'clock on a sad Saturday morning? No one.

By Sunday, my father is already boasting of his fine sense of business. Because there is a waiting list, it seems, and so many people desirous of possessing this model, these people are willing to pay quite a certain amount more than the car actually costs, for the privilege of immediate possession.

'Don't worry about me,' my father says. 'I know how to make a good business. Who needs a car anyhow? What for? You have to wash it, oil it, insure it, what for? What's wrong with the bus? Here, take a look at this cheque, you ever seen such a figure? Uh, scholar?'

And my mother, the master psychologist, smiles and says, 'I'll ring up Tzila. Maybe Sam will take us, we'll go to the beach.'

Glossary

page 55
toaster: small electric apparatus for making toast
fixing: repairing

page 56
lift: being driven from one place to another in a car
water-on-stone treatment: trying to persuade someone in a
    way that is no more successful than water attempting to
    break through the surface of a stone
stewed: stayed relaxing
pesach: the annual Jewish festival of Passover which
    celebrates the occasion when God spared the Hebrews in
    Egypt by 'passing over' the Israelites' houses which were
    marked with the blood of a lamb
flushed: hot and red in the face
toot: make a noise with its horn announcing its arrival

page 57
stealth: care, almost acting secretly

page 58
drops around: calls at the house, visits casually
latke: a pancake in Jewish cookery, often made of potatoes
feign: pretend

page 59
riveted: concentrated on, never moving away from
to brush up: to get back into practice and improve at the same
   time
ashen: very pale

page 60
c'mon (= come on)
Naah (= no)
nonchalant: very relaxed and unworried

page 61
brand-new: absolutely new, never used before

page 62
whips it up: drives it fast and expertly
bumper: the piece of metal or rubber which serves as a
   protection at the front and back of a car
Yom Kippur: the day of atonement or reconciliation in the
   Jewish calendar, observed as a day of fasting (when one eats
   no food)

page 63
fooled: unable to see the truth

Questions

1 How long did the father have his new car?
2 What happened when he brought the car home for the first
   time?
3 What was the father particularly proud of before he
   bought the new car?

4 What was special about the new car?
5 Why did the father decide to re-sell his new car?
6 What was his reaction to selling the car?
7 Try to describe the father as accurately as you can

Topics for discussion

1 In view of what happens do you think the mother was right in persuading the father to buy a car? Give your reasons.
2 Do you think the mother or the father had the stronger personality? Use some examples from the story to support your answer.
3 What is the role of the son in the story? What sort of person does he seem to be?
4 Try to describe a similar experience that has happened in your family.
5 What would you have done if the same thing had happened to you on the first day you took a new car home?
6 How far do you think the father was justified in re-selling the car?
7 What do you think was the author's main purpose in writing this story?

Graham Greene
A Day Saved

Graham Greene was born in 1904 and while still a
student at Oxford University had a book of poems
published. He later became a subeditor on The Times,
travelled widely, and wrote a number of books based
upon his experiences. He has worked as a film critic,
literary editor, and in the Foreign Office during the
Second World War. Greene is one of the most respected
of contemporary English writers and has written more
than thirty novels as well as several successful plays,
collections of essays and many short stories. Pe. haps his
best known novels are Brighton Rock (*1938*), The Power
and the Glory (*1940*), The Heart of the Matter (*1948*),
The End of the Affair (*1951*), The Quiet American
(*1958*) *and* The Comedians (*1966*). *Many of Greene's*
short stories, like this one, illustrate his acute
observation of people and places, and they frequently
incorporate a feeling of mystery and suspense.

I had stuck closely to him, as people say like a shadow.
But that's absurd. I'm no shadow. You can feel me,
touch me, hear me, smell me. I'm Robinson. But I had
sat at the next table, followed twenty yards behind
down every street, when he went upstairs I waited at the
bottom, and when he came down I passed out before
him and paused at the first corner. In that way I was
really like a shadow, for sometimes I was in front of him
and sometimes I was behind him.

Who was he? I never knew his name. He was short and ordinary in appearance and he carried an umbrella, his hat was a bowler;* and he wore brown gloves. But this was his importance to me: he carried something I dearly, despairingly wanted. It was beneath his clothes, perhaps in a pouch, a purse, perhaps dangling next to his skin. Who knows how cunning the most ordinary man can be? Surgeons can make clever insertions. He may have carried it even closer to his heart than the outer skin.

What was it? I never knew. I can only guess, as I might guess at his name, calling him Jones or Douglas, Wales, Canby, Fotheringay. Once in a restaurant I said 'Fotheringay' softly to my soup and I thought he looked up and round about him. I don't know. This is the horror I cannot escape: knowing nothing, his name, what it was he carried, why I wanted it so, why I followed him.

Presently we came to a railway bridge and underneath it he met a friend. I am using words again very inexactly. Bear with me. I try to be exact. I pray to be exact. All I want in the world is to know. So when I say he met a friend, I do not know that it was a friend, I know only that it was someone he greeted with apparent affection. The friend said to him, 'When do you leave?' He said, 'At two from Dover.'* You may be sure I felt my pocket to make sure the ticket was there.

Then his friend said, 'If you fly you will save a day.'

He nodded, he agreed, he would sacrifice his ticket, he would save a day.

I ask you, what does a day saved matter to him or to you? A day saved from what? for what? Instead of spending the day travelling, you will see your friend a day earlier, but you cannot stay indefinitely, you will travel home twenty-four hours sooner, that is all. But you will fly home and again save a day? Saving it from what, for what? You will begin work a day earlier, but you cannot work on indefinitely. It only means that you will cease work a day earlier. And then, what? You cannot die a day earlier. So you will realise perhaps how rash* it was of you to save a day, when you discover how you cannot escape those twenty-four hours you have so carefully preserved; you may push them forward and push them forward, but some time they must be spent, and then you may wish you had spent them as innocently as in the train from Ostend.*

But this thought never occurred to him. He said, 'Yes, that's true. It would save a day. I'll fly.' I nearly spoke to him then. The selfishness of the man. For that day which he thought he was saving might be his despair years later, but it was my despair at the instant. For I had been looking forward to the long train journey in the same compartment. It was winter, and the train would be nearly empty, and with the least luck we should be alone together. I had planned everything. I was going to talk to him. Because I knew nothing about him, I should begin in the usual way by asking whether he minded the window being raised a little or a little lowered. That would show him that we spoke the same language and he would probably be only too ready to talk, feeling himself in a foreign country; he would be grateful for any help I might be able to give him, translating this or that word.

Of course I never believed that talk would be enough. I should learn a great deal about him, but I believed that I should have to kill him before I knew all. I should have killed him, I think, at night, between the two stations which are the farthest parted, after the customs had examined our luggage and our passports had been stamped at the frontier, and we had pulled down the blinds and turned out the light. I had even planned what to do with his body, with the bowler hat and the umbrella and the brown gloves, but only if it became necessary, only if in no other way he would yield what I wanted. I am a gentle creature, not easily roused.*

But now he had chosen to go by aeroplane and there was nothing that I could do. I followed him, of course, sat in the seat behind, watched his tremulousness* at his first flight, how he avoided for a long while the sight of the sea below, how he kept his bowler hat upon his knees, how he gasped* a little when the grey wing tilted up like the arm of a windmill to the sky and the houses were set on edge. There were times, I believe, when he regretted having saved a day.

We got out of the aeroplane together and he had a small trouble with the customs. I translated for him. He looked at me curiously and said, 'Thank you'; he was – again I suggest that I know when all I mean is I assume by his manner and his conversation – stupid and good-natured, but I believe for a moment he suspected me, thought he had seen me somewhere, in a tube,* in a bus, in a public baths, below the railway bridge, on how many stairways. I asked him the time. He said, 'We put our clocks back an hour here,' and beamed with an absurd pleasure because he had saved an hour as well as a day.

I had a drink with him, several drinks with him. He was absurdly grateful for my help. I had beer with him at one place, gin at another, and at a third he insisted on my sharing a bottle of wine. We became for the time being friends. I felt more warmly towards him than towards any other man I have known, for, like love between a man and a woman, my affection was partly curiosity. I told him that I was Robinson; he meant to give me a card,* but while he was looking for one he drank another glass of wine and forgot about it. We were both a little drunk. Presently I began to call him Fotheringay. He never contradicted me and it may have been his name, but I seem to remember also calling him Douglas, Wales and Canby without correction. He was very generous and I found it easy to talk with him; the stupid are often companionable. I told him that I was desperate and he offered me money. He could not understand what I wanted.

I said, 'You've saved a day. You can afford to come with me tonight to a place I know.'

He said, 'I have to take a train tonight.' He told me the name of the town, and he was not surprised when I told him that I was coming too.

We drank together all that evening and went to the station together. I was planning, if it became necessary, to kill him. I thought in all friendliness that perhaps after all I might save him from having saved a day. But it was a small local train; it crept from station to station, and at every station people got out of the train and other people got into the train. He insisted on travelling third class and the carriage was never empty. He could not speak a word of the language and he simply curled up in his corner and slept; it was I who remained awake and had to listen to the weary painful gossip, a servant speaking of her mistress, a peasant woman of the day's market, a soldier of the Church, and a man who, I believe, was a tailor of adultery, wire-worms and the harvest of three years ago.

It was two o'clock in the morning when we reached the end of our journey. I walked with him to the house where his friends lived. It was quite close to the station and I had no time to plan or carry out any plan. The garden gate was open and he asked me in. I said no, I would go to the hotel. He said his friends would be pleased to put me up* for the remainder of the night, but I said no. The lights were on in a downstairs room and the curtains were not drawn. A man was asleep in a chair by a great stove and there were glasses on a tray, a decanter of whisky, two bottles of beer and a long thin bottle of Rhine wine. I stepped back and he went in and almost immediately the room was full of people. I could see his welcome in their eyes and in their gestures. There was a woman in a dressing-gown and a girl who sat with thin knees drawn up to her chin and three men, two of them old. They did not draw the curtains, though he must surely have guessed that I was watching them. The garden was cold; the winter beds* were furred with weeds. I laid my hand on some prickly bush. It was as if they gave a deliberate display of their unity and companionship. My friend – I call him my friend, but he was really no more than an acquaintance and was my friend only for so long as we both were drunk – sat in the middle of them all, and I could tell from the way his lips were moving that he was telling them many things which he had never told me. Once I thought I could detect from his lip movements, 'I have saved a day.' He looked stupid and good-natured and happy. I could not bear the sight for long. It was an impertinence to display himself like that to me. I have never ceased to pray from that moment that the day he saved may be retarded and retarded until eventually he suffers its eighty-six thousand four hundred seconds when he has the most desperate need, when he is following another as I followed him, closely as people say like a shadow, so that he has to stop, as I have had to stop, to reassure himself: You can smell me, you can touch me, you can hear me, I am not a shadow: I am Fotheringay, Wales, Canby, I am Robinson.

Glossary

page 68
bowler: the round, usually black hat which, with a folded
  umbrella, is the traditional symbol of the typical middle-
  class Englishman

Dover: one of the English ports on the Channel between England and France

page 69
rash: unwise, hasty
Ostend: a major port in Belgium

page 70
roused: moved to wild, uncontrolled actions
tremulousness: fear, shaking
gasped: made a noise expressing fear, a sudden intake of breath
tube: underground railway system (in London)
card: (visiting) card with a person's name and address on it

page 71
put me up: offer me a bed to sleep in.

page 72
beds: area in a garden kept for growing flowers

Questions

1 How did Robinson at first plan to kill the person he followed everywhere?
2 Why couldn't he carry out this plan?
3 Try to describe the person Robinson was following.
4 In what different ways is time important in the story?
5 'I thought in all friendliness that perhaps after all I might save him from having saved a day' (page 71). What does Robinson mean by this?

Topics for discussion

1 In what ways are you like (or unlike) Robinson?
2 Have you ever had a similar experience to the one Robinson describes? If so describe your experience as fully as you can.

3 '. . . like love between a man and a woman, my affection was partly curiosity' (page 70). How far do you think this is true?

4 '. . . the stupid are often companionable' (page 71). Can you think of occasions when this has seemed to be true?

5 In what ways did you enjoy (or not) this story?

Shiva Naipaul
A Man of Mystery

Shiva Naipaul is a West Indian writer who was born in Port-of-Spain, Trinidad in 1945. From 1964 he studied philosophy, psychology and finally Chinese at Oxford University, where he also began writing. Since then he has had a number of short stories and novels published, including Fireflies (*1970*), The Chip-Chip Gatherers (*1973*) and North of South (*1978*).

'A Man of Mystery' is set in the West Indies and tells of the rapid decline into drunkenness and finally death of the mysterious shoemaker and shoe-repairer, Mr Edwin Green, whose handsome and more sophisticated wife leaves him for a prosperous local doctor.

Grant Street could boast several business establishments: a grocery, a bookshop that sold chiefly Classic comics,* a café and, if you were sufficiently enthusiastic, the rum-shop around the corner (known as the Pax Bar) could also be included. On week-ends a coconut seller arrived with his donkey cart which he parked on the corner. The street's commercial character had developed swiftly but with the full approval of its residents. Commerce attracted strangers and the unbroken stream of traffic lent an air of excitement and was a source of pride. In time a group of steelbandsmen* had established themselves in one of the yards, adding thereby a certain finality and roundness to the physiognomy of the street. However, long before any of these

75

things had happened, Grant Street could point to Mr Edwin Green, 'shoemaker and shoe-repairer', whose workshop had been, until the recent immigrations, the chief landmark and point of reference.

From the first Mr Green had been considered by his neighbours to be different from themselves. There were good reasons for this. Grant Street lived an outdoor, communal life. Privacy was unknown and if anyone had demanded it he would have been laughed at. There were good reasons for this as well. The constant lack of privacy had led ultimately to a kind of fuzziness with regard to private property. No one was sure, or could be sure, what belonged to whom or who belonged to whom. When this involved material objects, like bicycles, there would be a fight. When it involved children, more numerous on Grant Street than bicycles, there was a feckless* tolerance of the inevitable doubts about paternity. Young men in pursuit of virility made false claims, while at other times the true father absconded.* No one worried, since in any case the child would eventually be absorbed into the life of the street. Romantic relationships, frankly promiscuous, were fleeting* rather than fragile, and the influx of strangers accelerated this tendency. Unfortunately, the results then were less happy. Grant Street was communal, but only up to a point, and any attachment one of its women might develop for a man from another street was looked upon with distaste. The inevitable child became the centre of a feud. Paternity in the stricter sense was of course not the issue. To which street did the child belong? It was over this problem that argument and acrimony raged.

Mr Green had been deposited in their midst like an alien body. Not only was he married, but his wife, a woman of half-Portuguese, half-Negro extraction, was pale-complexioned, good-looking and 'cultured'. In the late afternoon when Mr Green had closed his shop for the day, she would bring an easel out into the yard and paint for an hour. She had a fondness for sailing ships sinking in stormy seas and vases of flowers. The street, to begin with, had gathered solemnly around her and watched. She enjoyed their bewilderment.

'Lady, why you does paint when it so dark for?'

Mrs Green would stare seriously at her questioner.

'It's the light. There's a certain quality to this tropical twilight which I find so . . . so exhilarating.'

Her accent was 'foreign' and when she spoke her bosom heaved cinematically, suggesting a suppressed passion. This impressed her audience. Mrs Green also frequented the public library. On Saturday mornings the street saw her struggling under the weight of half a dozen books, the titles of which were conspicuously displayed. The women sitting on their front steps would laugh in awed disbelief and shout after her, 'Soon you go read up all the books they have in the library. You go have to begin writing them yourself then.' Mrs Green, looking martyred, would disappear into her yard.

All of this was curious enough, but what really intrigued the street was her attitude to Mr Green. They could not understand it. They were never seen together. During the day while he hammered in his shop, she was nowhere in evidence, while during her afternoon painting sessions, he in his turn seemed to have been swallowed up by the silence in their house. That silence was another cause for speculation. It was an unnatural, abnormal silence which many believed to be in some strange way a counterpart to the suppressed passion they thought they detected in Mrs Green's voice.

Nevertheless it was on her husband that the street's perplexity and wonder finally came to rest. The incongruities were not hard to find. Mr Green was spectacularly black, he was ugly, and he betrayed none of the outward signs of culture which his wife exhibited. Stated so baldly the problem was insoluble. That could not be tolerated. Therefore, the belief took shape that Mr Green was something other than he appeared to be. He was not a shoemaker at all; on the contrary, he was a man of the highest education who had chosen that lowly profession out of a profound and philosophic love for the 'simple life'. Mr Green, it was claimed, was in revolt against the hypocrisy and useless trappings* of modern civilization. Also for a time it was fashionable to uphold the theory that Mr Green spent much of his time in a trance,* but that was soon abandoned as being too improbable. Nevertheless it did not hinder his transformation into a man of mystery.

His shop became the centre of romance for children on the street. It was a small wooden hut situated at the front of the house (itself an enlarged hut on stilts*) under the shade of a tall tamarind tree. Above the door there was a sign which claimed he had the ability 'to fit all sizes and conform to all tastes'. This was a piece of rhetoric. As far as anyone could tell, Mr Green had not once been commissioned to make a pair of shoes; he simply repaired them. Inside there was a clutter of old, unreclaimed shoes overspread with dust. On a sagging worktable he arranged those recently brought in for repair and, always in the same place, an American trade magazine for the year 1950. Mr Green worked facing away from the light. He sat on a bench, holding several tiny nails between his teeth, occasionally extracting one which he would tack with exaggerated care into the shoe he was holding. After each such operation he examined the shoe from all angles and shook his head mournfully. The children crowding near him savoured the smells of leather in various stages of decomposition and bottles of glue which lay open beside him.

Gradually from his conversations with the children a

picture of his past was pieced together. He had lived in Brazil for many years where he had worked as a tapper* on a rubber plantation. There he had met his wife, the daughter of the overseer,* a hard and unfeeling man who kept his daughter a virtual prisoner and beat her regularly and viciously. She had begged him to take her away – he was the only foreigner working on the plantation – and together they had fled to British Guiana where she had borne him a child, a daughter. They had named her Rosa. The overseer having by that time repented, and they being extremely poor, the child was sent back to Brazil to live with her grandfather. In the meantime, they had saved sufficient money to buy a house and it was thus they had come to Trinidad and to Grant Street. His one sadness in life was never to have seen his daughter – 'a full and grown woman now' – and it was only the hope of seeing her again that kept him 'alive'.

This was a far cry* from the picture that had been built up, and while no one really believed the story, it did have its attractions. Therefore the street pretended to believe that it believed Mr Green. He made their task easy. He was everything they expected him to be: kind, gentle, and a little sad. His eccentricities pleased them, especially his dress for occasions, which was invariable and immaculate. He wore a starched and ironed white tropical suit and a cork hat, and when he began taking the children for walks the men lounging on the corner murmured as he passed them, 'Make way for the Governor, everybody make way for the Governor.'

On his Sunday walks Mr Green took the children to the zoo and botanical gardens. They went early in the afternoon, marching in military formation behind Mr Green, who walked stiffly ahead of them. When they had come to the highest point in the Queen's Park Savannah,* he would gather the children more informally about him and show them the sea and the ships in the harbour. 'The Brazils,' he would say, 'lie in that direction, and Venezuela, which from certain points you can see on a clear day, in that.' His arms extended in a sweep that embraced the harbour and the glittering sea beyond. When this ritual had been performed, they crossed the road to the zoo. He appeared to have a taste only for those animals he had seen in the wild. 'They call those jaguars? Who they trying to fool?* I'll tell you about a jaguar I saw in Brazil one time.' And he would relate a long and tortuous tale. The birds, though, were his favourites and he was at his most lyrical* when talking about them. 'They call those parrots? I've seen them in the wild. The colours of the rainbow and more besides. Wonderful creatures. They belong in the jungle,' and adjusting his hat he led them to the alligator pond, as if what he had just seen had been calculated to offend him personally.

Afterwards, they went to the botanical gardens, which, at six o'clock, would be nearly empty. There he allowed them to rest, and while they sprawled* on the grass he wandered along the gravelled paths, staring up at the trees, occasionally bending close to read the labels attached to the trunks. Sometimes, perhaps struck by the sudden recall of an incident or a landscape long forgotten, he left off his examination of the trees and gazed abstractedly at the flag flapping limply over the roof of the Governor's house, itself hidden by a bandstand and the clumps of trees growing thickly nearby. At such times it was not difficult for the children to make believe that he was indeed the Governor, and that these were his private grounds. There was something truly proprietorial about Mr Green as he stood there, oblivious of their presence, hostage to some troubling recollection. However, a gust of wind through the trees or a fight among the children and the melancholy would be set aside, to be resurrected and resumed the following Sunday.

His shadow stretched out before him on the path, the harshness of his dress muted in the softer light, he led them through an avenue of trees to the greenhouses where the more exotic exhibits were on display and there showed them insect-devouring plants, fruit one bite of which sufficed to kill a man, and a tree that 'bled'. Mr Green lingered over these things longer than the children cared for. The botanical gardens, so alien, so distinct, seemed hardly to connect with the street they had left three hours before. It was a swept, ordered profusion, a region of shadow on cut grass and strange fruit made stranger still by Mr Green's heady* fascination for malignancies they did not understand and which appalled and frightened them. Some of the children cried, but Mr Green, ignoring, or perhaps ignorant of their distress, touched and smelled everything, delighting in the heat and spray of water from the pipes, his suit and helmet tinted green by the light filtering through the vines that crept up the sides of the glass and spread out over the roof. He would leave only when one of the caretakers looked in and told them it was time to go.

If these visits were not the undiluted pleasures they ought to have been, there were some advantages to be had in associating with Mr Green. He was a skilled carpenter and built stools and chairs and desks which he gave to the children. However, the most prized of all his accomplishments were the telephones he was able to make out of bits of wire and old tins. This sustained his popularity and at the same time it allowed him to continue his excursions to the zoo and botanical gardens.

Time having smoothed the rougher edges, the street learned to accept the Greens, bestowing on them the respect that springs from incomprehension. Crowds no longer gathered to watch Mrs Green paint, and although the men lounging on the corner still shouted, 'Here comes the Governor,' when Mr Green appeared dressed in his white suit, it was done less from malice than a desire to acknowledge his presence. Yet the Greens did come to have one thing in common with their neighbours: they shared their unchanging way of life. In that life, no one ever got richer or poorer; there were no dramatic successes or, for that matter, dramatic failures; no one was ever in serious trouble. Basically, they were cowards. Now and again Grant Street spawned* a prodigy, a policeman for instance, but that was considered an aberration and did not happen often. Nevertheless, unheroic as it undoubtedly was, the street did have its heroes: the man in the Western* who, flying in the face of the odds, conquers all, and his corollary, the loser, riding off, but with dignity, into the sunset.

The Greens succumbed to this pattern. The shoeshop maintained a steady trickle of customers; Mrs Green continued to paint ships in distress and vases of flowers; the same silence swallowed now the husband, now the wife; and the tamarind tree, a prisoner of its own maturity, grew no taller. The changes Grant Street knew centred on the succession of carnivals, of births, and of deaths. Marriage, like the policeman, was an aberration that occurred infrequently. Ephemeral groups of children called Charlie and Yvonne and Sheila gathered round Mr Green and were introduced to the wonders of the zoo and botanical gardens and they cried as their predecessors had done. Mr Green, in his turn, saw them grow up, become mothers and putative* fathers, fading away from him to the street corners and front steps of hovels.*

Therefore when Mrs Green started work as a receptionist to a doctor it was considered almost an infringement of the established order, and when he was seen to come for her* in the mornings and bring her back in the afternoons, it amounted to a disturbance of the peace. It soon became apparent that her suppressed passion had found an outlet. All the symptoms were there. When the doctor brought her back in the afternoon they talked long and earnestly in the car before he left, and Mrs Green, who, though distant had always been friendly, now abandoned her friendliness altogether. One change led to another. The painting sessions stopped and so did the visits to the library on Saturday mornings. From these occurrences were dated the commercialization that was to sweep* Grant Street, as if there were some species of sympathetic magic at work connecting the two sets of events. And it certainly was the case that hard on the heels of* Mrs Green's liaison the Pax Bar and grocery first made their appearance. Mr Green alone seemed unaware of what was happening. He worked in his shop as usual, smiled benignly at the children and took them out for walks. Unfortunately it was noted that he had recently begun to make more telephones than he had ever done. Mr Green's sadness ceased to be speculative. The street had its standards. There were limits to what anyone could do, and one of the unspoken rules in their relationship with Mr Green was that their standards did not apply to him: he had a role to fulfil. They felt not merely that his wife was 'wronging' him, but more peculiarly, that her manner of doing it was sordid. For them, morality was a matter of form, 'style', and they did not approve of Mrs Green's style.

Grant Street's commercialization proceeded apace, and in the rush of cars and business and the sounds of the steelband, the Greens receded. The steelband was the street's pride and had rapidly become the focus of its loyalties. They practised every night and were good enough to merit being recorded. The radio spread their fame and eventually even the American tourists came to marvel at the men who could produce such sweet and coherent sounds from oil drums. Mr Green, his accomplishments thrown into shadow by the influx of visitors, was deserted by his youthful congregation. The telephones which he made in increasing quantities lost their market and lay in untidy heaps on top of the trade magazine for 1950. He had to entice the children into the shop and as before tried to talk to those who did come about his life in Brazil and the daughter he longed to see, but they were impatient and not interested in these stories. Formerly, they had begged him for his telephones and compliance had had to be dragged out of him. Now to hold them in his shop he had to promise instruments of greater sophistication. The next day he would be sure to see his efforts abandoned in the gutter* outside his house or being kicked along the street. He stopped making telephones and on Sundays he took his walks alone. One or two people remembered to say, 'Here comes the Governor', but it was done without any enthusiasm, and Mr Green to avoid them went another way.

One morning some workmen arrived and they produced the first noises to come from the Greens. A crowd gathered on the pavement to watch. The house was being pulled down. Mr Green was detached. He worked in his shop all day amid the crashing of timber and galvanized iron sheets. The doctor arrived to supervise the demolition, leaving later with Mrs Green and two trunks, an action sufficiently daring to mollify* the neighbours. There was no silence for Mr Green to return to that night. The house was already roofless and instead he went to the Pax Bar.

Everyone there recognized him and looked up with

unconcealed surprise when he went in. He bought half a
bottle of rum and sat alone in a corner. He wore his
white suit and did not remove his cork hat. Towards
morning Mr Green shook himself and got up a little
unsteadily from his chair. He fixed his hat more firmly
on his head and felt his way across the room, holding on
to the sides of tables and backs of chairs in his path. The
few remaining drunks eyed him disconsolately. 'Good
night. Governor.' Mr Green went out into the dark,
empty street. A chain of red beacon lights, punctured
the blackness of the hills. Grant Street was unreal in the
stillness. Gazing up at the street lamps and the shuttered
houses he walked slowly back to the workshop. He fum-
bled for a long time before he found his keys. There was
no light in the shop and he lit a candle. Half-made telephones littered the bench and table. He picked up one,
held the receiver to his ear and laughed. The trade
magazine caught his eye. He leafed through* it, glanc-
ing at the advertisements. The Baltimore Shoe Cor-
poration claimed to be able to 'fit all sizes and conform to
all tastes'. Mr Green laughed again and put the magazine back on the table. He closed the door, snuffed* the
candle and went to sleep on the floor.

When he awoke the demolition men were already at
work. The doctor was giving them instructions. Mr
Green examined his suit in the semi-darkness. It had
changed colour, and circular brown patches showed
where rum had fallen on it the night before. He started
brushing it, then, frowning, he gave up the attempt. He
opened late and worked until lunch-time, when he
closed the shop and went to the Pax Bar. It was the last
time Edwin Green, 'shoemaker and shoe-repairer', ever
opened for business.

It was a small house and in three days the demolition
was complete. The street salvaged what it could from

the piles of timber laid out on the pavement. There was no one to stop them except the doctor, and even he, after an argument in which he called them 'carrion crows',* allowed them to take what they wished. The new house took shape slowly. Grant Street had never seen anything like it. It was large and rambling* in the Californian fashion, surrounded by a lawn and fenced in from the street. The outside walls were painted a bright pink, and wooden louvres* were used instead of windows. There were wrought iron gates surmounted by wrought iron lanterns. But by far the most impressive innovation was the chimney on the roof.

Mrs Green returned when it was finished. She behaved as if she had come to the street for the first time. In the afternoons she watered the lawn while the doctor fussed with the potted plants and orchids which hung from the eaves.* Mr Green was banished to his reservation.* His shop had not been touched and stood in ramshackle* and bizarre opposition to the modernity that seemed poised to devour it. The street had long ago surrendered its illusions about him. The evidence to the contrary was too overwhelming, and anyway they did not need these illusions. Mr Green's fall had been public and obvious, and any private sorrow which he might still have had could not compensate for or hide his humiliation. Now all they could see was the physical shell whose disintegration they studied with a passive morbidity. Grant Street had a clear conscience. It had expressed its sympathy for Mr Green and its horror of what his wife was doing. There were many other things demanding their attention.

Mr Green lived in the shop. His revelries* in the Pax Bar ended late in the evening, and as he crept down the street on his way home he sang noisily, pausing to swear when his steps stuttered uncontrollably. Occasionally he stumbled and fell on the roadway and then he would lie

there for some minutes without moving. Sometimes he
urinated as he lay there, taking fresh swigs* from the
bottle he always carried with him. He delivered his final
orations outside the shop, laughing and cursing in turn
as he kicked at the door until it gave way. Then, suddenly, he would fall silent and leaning against the fence,
stare at the freshly watered lawn and the curtains in the
new house drawn tight and secure. At noon the next day
he emerged, his suit tattered and frayed beyond recog-
nition, the cork hat dented and twisted at an odd angle
on his head, to make the journey once again to the Pax
Bar. Mr Green's metamorphosis had been quickly absorbed into the landscape. The world had come to Grant
Street and it would take more than the ragings of a
drunken man to disturb them.

Sunday afternoon was hot. The men on the corner had
sought the shade of the bookshop and in the yards children played and the women sat on their front steps fan-
ning themselves and gossiping. The steelband
maundered* sleepily to itself; the Pax Bar would not
open until evening. Grant Street was in limbo.*
   Tamarinds were in season and several children were
collecting the fruit that had fallen off the tree and littered the yard in front of the shoe shop. Mr Green
watched them from the doorway. His eyes were red and
he blinked painfully in the harsh light. He reached for
the bottle of rum on his work table, uncorked it and
drank some. With a faint smile and still holding the
bottle he approached the children gathering the tamarinds. He picked up a handful and offered it to one of
the smaller girls. She shook her head and backing away
began to cry. The other children retreated, dropping the
fruit they had collected. Mr Green laughed, and stepped
out on to the street. He looked at the house. The louvres
were opened and even in the gloom* he could see that

the walls were covered with pictures. One stood out. It was a painting of a ship with only its rigging* visible, on the verge of being totally annihilated by a mountainous sea. He threw the tamarinds in the gutter and started up the street. His walk was studied and tentative. The urine stains on his trousers showed clearly. He took another sip* from the bottle and shielding his eyes from the sun he gazed up at the sky. There were only a few clouds about, and they were small and white. He quickened his pace when he saw the coconut seller turn the corner with his donkey cart.

The donkey, a shaggy,* morose, under-fed creature, had been tethered* in a patch of weeds. Mr Green stopped to examine it. He passed his hands over its shanks* and patted it. The men in the shelter of the bookshop laughed. Mr Green turned to address them. 'Do you call this a donkey? Poor creature. I've seen them in the wild . . .' The rest of what he said was lost in their laughter. The coconut seller advanced on him. 'Mister, you better leave my donkey alone, or you go know what.' He traced patterns in the air with his cutlass. 'Friend, I was only pointing out . . .' The coconut seller spluttered into obscenity and Mr Green, shaking his head sadly, drank some more rum and walked away.

On the Queen's Park Savannah people were playing cricket and football and horses were cantering on the exercise track near the racecourse. Families out for their Sunday walk paraded amiably on the perimeter. Mr Green sat on a bench under a tree and stared at them, eyes half-closed. A clock struck four. He was tired and sleepy and beads of sweat watered his face and arms. An attack of nausea frittered* itself away, but the tiredness, reinforcing itself, would not go. He opened his eyes. There was a breeze and the dust was rising in clouds, hiding the horses and people. The colours of the sky and

grass melted and footballers and cricketers wandered
through a golden, jellied haze.* A voice unattached to a
body spoke near him, then receded. Someone tapped
him on the shoulder. A dog played round his heels and
barked from many miles away. Beyond the Savannah
the sea was a sheet of light. The sun fled behind a cloud
and the sea was grey and rose up to devour him. He
shuddered. For a moment the disoriented world re-
grouped, but it needed all his energy and all his will to
keep it that way. He let it dissolve and shatter.* The
rum was everywhere, flowing from chimneys and lanterns and tumescent* seas, soaking his clothes. He
kicked feebly and the bottle rolled into the dust. He got
up. The ground shivered. He swam to the iron railings
protecting the Savannah from the road. Another dog
barked, a herald of the loneliness descending on all sides.
Someone said, '. . . back in time for dinner,' and someone
laughed. Weariness called on him to surrender, but he
was already on the road, creeping between the cars, and
not far away was a refuge of shaded green. A flag
danced in the sky. The brown, lifeless hills wavered. A
gust of wind blew through the trees; blossoms floated in
the air, trees and trunks and labels whirled towards him.
The tree-lined avenue was cooler and he was startled by
his reflection looming up to meet him out of the foliage.
In a moment he was inside. There was a sound of spray,
and water dripped on to his hat and trickled down his
face. The desolation deepened. Stalks and flowers
stumbled in the effort to make themselves seen. He noticed the green light flowing through the glass, becoming one with his nausea, and he tried to remember
why the children had cried. The tree that bled. He
moved towards it, but darkness closed in, confounding
his desire, bringing with it the smell of fruit even
stranger than those he had described, of flower-laden
jungles and muddy rivers, landscapes of the mind more

real than any he had roamed.* Then, mercifully, there was only the darkness.

When the caretaker found him he had been dead for an hour.

Two days later Mr Green was buried in the Mucurapo cemetery. His body, contrary to custom, had been kept in the funeral home, returning to Grant Street for the brief religious service which was held in the drawing room* of the new house. Some hitherto unsuspected relations of Mr Green turned up and wept, but no one from the street was allowed in. They gathered on the pavement and stared through the louvres at the coffin.

The procession did not have far to travel and a sombre crowd of neighbours walked behind the hearse* to the cemetery. Mrs Green drove in a car. The sky clouded and it began to rain, delaying the burial. It was already dark by the time it was completed and the few limp wreaths had been scattered on the grave.

Within a month the workshop was pulled down – it took one morning to do the job – and for days afterwards the children played with the unreclaimed shoes that had been thrown in the gutter. The tide of grass invaded the spot where the shop had been, and the fence was extended.

Grant Street prospered. The borough council gave it concrete pavements and running water, and the Central Government, a sewage system. Commercialization had stimulated its ambitions and several of the residents built new houses, none of course as grand as the Enriques' (Mrs Green had remarried), but all with pretensions to modernity. The grocery had become a supermarket, the café a restaurant; and the steelband went on tours to the Bahamas and United States. Romantic relationships were regularized, and there were even a few marriages. Children were still numerous, but the index had changed: they were more numerous than motor cars.

The street had undergone a series of changes that went beyond carnival and birth and death, and this had brought nostalgia. Grant Street had acquired a past whose sharpness had been softened by the passage of time and now glowed with a gentle light. Those who were no longer there or had died shared that softness and were transfigured by it. Mr Green had left no physical reminder of his presence to trouble them and as a result his legend revived. His style of death, a memorial to his dreams, was beyond reproach, and in the end it redeemed him. Put in another way, in terms of the Westerns Grant Street loved, he had ridden into the sunset.*

Glossary

page 75
comics: papers consisting mainly of cartoon serials, usually designed for children
steelbandsmen: groups who make typically West Indian music by beating oil drums

page 76
feckless: careless, irresponsible
absconded: didn't reveal his identity
fleeting: brief, constantly changing

page 78
trappings: things that people consider to be a necessary part of modern life (here, for example, social status, education, possessions, money)
trance: dreamlike, mystical state of mind
stilts: wooden poles to raise it above the ground

Shiva Naipaul

page 79
tapper: man who extracts the liquid from a rubber tree
overseer: supervisor, foreman
far cry: very different
Queen's Park Savannah: a large park in Port-of-Spain which
    contains the botanical gardens and a race course

page 80
fool: deceive
lyrical: expressive and enthusiastic
sprawled: lay relaxing, spread out

page 81
heady: exciting, intoxicating

page 82
spawned: gave birth to
Western: film of cowboys and frontier life in the American
    West
putative: presumed, supposed
hovels: very poor accommodation, often primitive huts

page 83
come for her: collect her in his car
sweep: completely dominate and rapidly change
hard on the heels of: very soon after

page 84
gutter: small channel at the edge of the road to carry water
    away
mollify: pacify their anger

page 85
leafed through: turned the pages quickly without
    concentrating
snuffed: put out, extinguished

page 86
carrion crows: large black birds which feed on dead flesh
rambling: spread out over a large area

wooden louvres: wooden shutters fixed on the outside of a
    house as protection against the weather
eaves: overhanging parts of the roof
reservation: an area of land where underprivileged people are
    forced to live to preserve their own culture and way of
    life (e.g. the Indian reservations in North America)
ramshackle: in need of repair, broken down
revelries: noisy drinking sessions

page 87
swigs: large drinks
maundered: played lazily
in limbo: floating in a dream-like state waiting for something
    to happen
gloom: semi-darkness

page 88
rigging: system of ropes controlling the mast and sails of a ship
sip: a very small drink
shaggy: long-haired and untidy looking
tethered: tied up
shanks: lower part of its legs
frittered: gradually disappeared

page 89
jellied haze: sticky, heavy mist
shatter: break up into many pieces
tumescent: swollen

page 90
roamed: wandered about without any real purpose
drawing room: formal reception room
hearse: vehicle transporting the coffin

page 91
he had ridden into the sunset: he had died in the same
    classically romantic way that many Western films
    traditionally end

Questions

1 What sort of street was Grant Street at the beginning of the story?
2 Why did Mr Green marry his wife?
3 What were the principal differences between Mr Green and his wife?
4 How did the other residents of Grant Street regard Mrs Green when she and her husband first came to live there?
5 What were Mrs Green's main hobbies?
6 'His shop became the centre of romance for children on the street' (page 78). Why was this?
7 What did Mr Green do apart from repairing shoes?
8 Why did Mr Green particularly like visiting the botanical gardens?
9 How does the character of the street change during the story?
10 How did Mr Green react to the commercialization of Grant Street?
11 Where did Mr Green die?
12 'Children were still numerous, but the index had changed: they were more numerous than motor cars' (page 91). What does the author want to suggest by this?

Topics for discussion

1 'Therefore, the belief took shape that Mr Green was something other than he appeared to be' (page 78). How far do you think this is true?
2 To what extent do you feel sympathy for Mr Green?
3 Can you see any justification for what Mrs Green did?
4 How do you think you would have reacted in Mr Green's circumstances?
5 Do you think Mr Green really liked children?
6 What do you think was the real cause of Mr Green's death?

V. S. Pritchett
The Educated Girl

V. S. Pritchett was born in 1900 and is still actively
writing in London where he lives today. He is very well
known and admired both as a writer and as an eminent
critic of other people's work. He has written many
novels including Mr Belunde (*1951*), Dead Man Leading
(*1957*) *and* The Key to my Heart (*1963*) *and his*
numerous short stories have appeared in collections like
The Sailor and the Saint *and* When my Girl Comes
Home.

'The Educated Girl' is a charming and amusing story
about the problems a new young waitress causes the
regular customers at Bianchi's restaurant. It also
demonstrates Pritchett's strong visual sense and his
liking for the sound of people's speech.

July. There was a new waitress at Bianchi's.

'Justine!' Mrs Bianchi called, from her desk at the
doorway of the little restaurant. 'Number four.'

The new waitress slipped her sandals back on and
walked very slowly, her head lowered and a handful of
straight fair hair hanging forward over her face, expos-
ing one large, still, strong grey eye to the customer at
table number four.

'We got her from the Art School,' Mrs Bianchi comfortably explained to an old customer.

'Yes,' said Mr Bianchi, making a despairing distinc-
tion. 'Mrs Bianchi got her. Staff is the big headache.'*

'It's pocket money for them,' said Mrs Bianchi wistfully, her eyes going very small.

'She's an educated girl,' said Mr Bianchi suicidally.

'You can't pay the wages,' said Mrs Bianchi. 'They come out of the slums of Naples,' Mrs Bianchi opened up sharply on Mr Bianchi, 'and they want the earth.'

'She's got her shoes off again,' said Mr Bianchi.

'She's British,' said Mrs Bianchi who was enormously British.

The new waitress stood by the table waiting for the customer to give her order. The customer was wearing a wide-brimmed red straw hat.

'Good morning,' the customer said, 'I think I will have . . .'

'My sister has a hat like that,' the waitress said. 'She got it at Bourne's. Did you get yours at Bourne's? I want to get one. Hers is yellow, pale yellow. She can't wear strong colours.'

The woman took off her glasses.

'I should like to have an omelette,' the woman said.

'She wears hers with grey,' the waitress said. Her voice was slow, clear and low like a funeral march.

'I tell her to try putting a band round it, nothing fancy, just a plain silk band round it and tie it under her chin – well one could do that, couldn't one? Or let it fall back on your shoulders – it wouldn't suit me but *you* could do it. You have got to be the type. Cheese or ham?'

'A mushroom omelette,' said the woman coldly.

'I can't eat them,' said the waitress, speaking with one foot in the grave. 'It must be an allergy. I love picking them, but I can't eat them. I was reading a book where it said that four hundred people have died in France in the last three years from eating them.'

Her single eye gazed at the woman's hat.

'False Blushers,* I expect,' said the waitress. 'Many people confuse the real Blusher with the False.'

The woman did not answer.

Slowly the new waitress walked to Mrs Bianchi's desk.

'A plain omelette,' she said to Mrs Bianchi. 'She was wearing a green cloche* yesterday. She doesn't speak.'

Mr Bianchi, whose job it was to stand near Mrs Bianchi and welcome the customers, closed his eyes with pain. Mrs Bianchi caught* this and took a full, carnivorous look at Mr Bianchi. He was a green-faced man; a chicken bone with not much left on it that she might have picked up and had a chew at from time to time. She resumed the usual expression of satisfied consternation that was set between her thick black brows and her black moustache. In getting the kind of girl Mr Bianchi would never run after,* Mrs Bianchi had frightened herself.

At number seven, Mr Rougemont from the Museum had just sat down and was unloading his pockets. He propped a book against the water jug.

'Soup,' he said to the new waitress.

'Soup?' she said.

'Yes, soup,' said Mr Rougemont.

She was trying to read the title of his book. He closed it and stared at her.

'On a hot day like this?' said the new waitress.

Heavily made and with a scholarly readiness for controversy, he asked: 'Does soup have to be hot? Isn't there such a thing as cold soup?'

'Yes,' said the girl. 'But it is not good for ulcers.'

Mr Rougemont put his book aside and with a fighter's grin of pleasure looked around to see what the audience was like. There were few customers, the nearest was a woman in the red hat.

'Who put that nonsense into your head?' said Mr Rougemont.

'Lettuce, as well,' said the girl. 'The doctor will not allow my father to eat lettuce.'

'Ho!' exclaimed Mr Rougemont with a glance at the red hat. 'I should think not. We are not rabbits.'

The red hat lowered its face.

'Or salads,' said the girl. 'Americans are always eating salads and they have ulcers.'

'Yes, but I am not an American,' said Mr Rougemont.

'You have thick white hair,' said the unsmiling girl.

'Bring me some cold soup and stop generalizing, girl – now don't go away, wait for the rest of the order.'

'There is not cold consommé,' said the melancholy girl. 'There is salami. Or *pâté de foie*, if you're not afraid of rich things. My father . . .'

'Do I look ill?'

'Egg mayonnaise . . .'

'Would your father mind if I had a sardine? I don't want a sardine, but let us say your father is about to have a sardine – what would that do to him?'

'Give him gout,'* said the girl. 'Like tomatoes and spinach. But he could eat herring.'

'Ulcers, gout,' called Mr Rougemont loudly to the woman in the red hat. 'Is this a restaurant or a hospital? Now, don't go away. Veal – what is the matter with the veal?'

'It's done with mushrooms.'

The woman in the red hat spoke across two tables to Mr Rougemont. 'The young lady tells me,' the woman said in a polished way, 'that four hundred people died in France last month . . .'

'In the last three years,' the waitress corrected.

'. . . from eating mushrooms.'

'That is what I will have,' called out the robust Mr Rougemont. 'And I'll have the potatoes boiled and peas.'

'*Petits pois*,' said the girl in a docile voice.

'I said peas,' said Mr Rougemont.

'I said,' said the girl.

'You didn't,' said Mr Rougemont. 'You said *petits pois*. Peas are one thing, *petits pois* another.'

'Yes,' said the girl. 'The only peas we have are *petits pois.*'

The girl's one eye stared at Mr Rougemont. His eyes stared at her and went very blue. He had a very white forehead and a large vein began to swell in the middle of it.

'Send Mr Bianchi to me!' he shouted.

Mr Bianchi came down from the desk to the table.

'Is there anything wrong, Mr Rougemont?' said Mr Bianchi, snapping his fingers at the girl who went back to the desk.

'Where did you get that Cyclops?' said Mr Rougemont.

'Cyclops?' said Mr Bianchi, picking up the menu and looking at it.

'No, no, not on there, Bianchi – the girl. With one eye.'

Mr Bianchi turned and stood with his back to Mrs Bianchi, moved his hands a little, wagged his shoulders a little, rolled his eyeballs in Mrs Bianchi's direction.

'She talks like a hearse,'* said Mr Rougemont.

'Five days and she kicks her sandals off. Customers do not like it,' Mr Bianchi whispered. 'Give me your order. I will see to it.'*

The girl now came with a plain omelette and put it on the table before the woman with the red hat. Mr Rougemont saw it.

'No!' he shouted getting to his feet. 'No, madam, refuse to eat it. You ordered a mushroom omelette. Make her take it back. Waitress, take it back.'

The woman hesitated. Mr Rougemont looked around at the two or three customers.

V. S. Pritchett

'Are you eating what you ordered?' he cried.

'There was no answer.

'Cowards,' muttered Mr Rougemont.

'Mr Rougemont,' pleaded Mr Bianchi, touching his arm.

'No,' said Mr Rougemont, going to the woman's table and taking away the omelette.

'You will drop it,' said the waitress in a sad voice.

'Give it to me,' said Mr Bianchi, taking it from him.

'I'm in a hurry,' said the woman. 'It doesn't matter.'

The waitress took the omelette and went away with it.

'Bring it back,' called the woman and stood up herself and got the omelette back.

'They owe you an apology, madam,' said Mr Rougemont, quietening and sitting down at his table once more.

'Now give me your order, Mr Rougemont. I am very sorry. We have a very nice egg mayonnaise, or the *pâté de foie*. A little *pâté* ...'

'I said soup,' said Mr Rougemont, sulking.*

'Or tomato salad.'

'Don't you start, Bianchi, for God's sake,' said Mr Rougemont, getting his breath.

'Shouting is bad for his digestion,' said the girl in a low sorrowful voice, from a distance.

'Soup,' hissed Bianchi at the girl. 'Quick.'

'Roast veal, potatoes and peas,' said Mr Rougemont, exhausted. Then he said: 'Where is Rosa, Bianchi?'

'She left,' sighed Mr Bianchi.

'And Maria?'

'They both left,' said Mr Bianchi.

'Why did they leave?'

Mr Bianchi shrugged* and sighed.

'And the big one, with the golden hair? She was heading for trouble.'

'Lucia,' said Mr Bianchi in a low voice, with a glance back at Mrs Bianchi. 'She's still around.' He nodded to the street.

'Ah,' nodded Mr Rougemont knowingly.

'Yes,' admitted Mr Bianchi, 'Mrs Bianchi does not like Italian girls. So – we carry on.'

'Not with that one, you don't, Bianchi,' said Mr Rougemont. 'I will tell you something about her. People say witchcraft has died out. It hasn't. She's a witch – you be careful, the northern type. I know them. They haunt* you.'

'Ha! ha!' said Mr Bianchi feebly, looking happier. 'How is Mrs Rougemont? Well, I hope?'

'Of course not,' said Mr Rougemont. 'I say, they haunt you.'

Soon Mr Rougemont's food was brought to him. He buttered a roll and nodded cheerfully to the woman with the red hat.

'Still alive?' he said.

The woman smiled with contentment.

'I've been coming here for years,' he said.

'So have I,' she said.

'I'm afraid this one will finish Bianchi,' he said. 'She has a voice like a crypt.'*

Presently he saw the girl standing near and watching him eat.

'You get in a temper. It heats the blood, it's bad for the heart,' said the girl gazing at him. 'An income tax collector shouted at my father because he wouldn't pay his taxes. I don't know what he was going to do to him, have him arrested ...'

'No,' said Mr Rougemont equably, with his mouth full. 'They don't arrest. They detain.'

'And my father said, "If you go on shouting and banging the table like that you'll drop dead".'

'And I suppose he did,' said Mr Rougemont genially.

'Not then,' said the girl. 'Later.'

Mr Rougemont put down his knife and fork and gazed at her.

'You have an unusual interest in death in your family,' said Mr Rougemont, frowning.

'Yes,' said the girl. 'My brother . . .'

'No,' said Mr Rougemont, holding up his hand. 'Bring me a fish knife and fork.'

'Are you having fish now?' said the girl.

'No,' said Mr Rougemont. 'But I like to eat at a table that is properly laid. How do you know I mightn't have wanted fish?'

The girl brought the fish knife and fork.

'Thank you,' he said. 'And another wine glass. Not for me. I already have one.' He nodded at the vacant place on the other side of the table.

'For my friend,' he said.

'You are expecting a friend?'

'Now, do as I tell you. He will want knives, forks, a side plate, dessert spoon.'

The girl got them and waited. Mr Rougemont went on eating.

'Good. Now, take his order,' he said.

'Is he coming soon?' asked the girl.

'He is there *now*,' said Mr Rougemont, still eating. 'Take it. He is impatient and hungry.'

The new waitress brushed her hair back from her face and two grey eyes looked like stones at Mr Rougemont.

'Look after him well,' said Mr Rougemont. 'Because I shall bring him again tomorrow.'

A very thin smile came to the lips of the girl. She took her pad and wrote a few lines on it. It was Mr Rougemont's bill.

Mr Rougemont did not come to Bianchi's for a week or more. But when he did the new waitress came to his table.

'I liked your friend very much,' she said to him. 'He's been in several times.'

'What?' said Mr Rougemont.

'He's taking me out* on Thursday,' she said. 'What are you having today? There is cold soup – but the weather's changed, hasn't it?'

Glossary

page 95
headache: problem

page 97
False Blushers: the name for a plant that looks like a genuine
    edible mushroom, but is in fact poisonous
cloche: a type of close-fitting hat
caught: noticed
run after: be attracted by

page 98
gout: a painful swelling of the legs

page 99
hearse: vehicle used to transport a coffin to its burial place
see to it: make sure you get what you ordered

page 100
sulking: showing childlike anger
shrugged: made a gesture with his shoulders to show he didn't
    know the reason why they had left

page 101
haunt: frequently appear to people in the form of
    disembodied spirits or ghosts
crypt: underground burial place in a church

page 103
taking me out: inviting me to something.

Questions

1 What does the writer mean by, 'Mr Rougemont put his book aside and with a fighter's grin of pleasure looked round to see what the audience was like' (page 97)?
2 Describe what sort of person the story suggests Mr Rougemont is?
3 What kind of restaurant does Bianchi's seem to be? What is its main problem?
4 What is Mr Bianchi's particular job in the restaurant?
5 Does Mr Bianchi or his wife really seem to be in charge of the restaurant? Give reasons for your answer.
6 What sort of girls do the Bianchis seem to have as waitresses?
7 Why do they leave the restaurant?
8 Why does the waitress say, 'He's taking me out on Thursday' (page 103)?

Topics for discussion

1 Which of the characters in the story do you find most likeable? Give your reasons.
2 How far do you find the new waitress really believes her descriptions of the dangers of eating various foods, or are they simply designed to annoy the customers?
3 What would you have done if the waitress had brought you something you hadn't ordered?
4 How far do you feel Mr Rougemont is justified in muttering 'cowards' on page 100?
5 How would you react to the general situation if you had been a regular customer in Bianchi's restaurant?
6 If you were the owner of a restaurant what would you particularly want it to be well known for?
7 If you were choosing a new waitress for your restaurant, what would be the main qualities you would look for?

Murray Bail
Life of the Party

Murray Bail, who was born in Adelaide in 1941, is
rapidly becoming one of the best known of the new
generation of Australian short story writers. He began
writing in 1965 and ten years later his first collection of
short stories was published under the title
Contemporary Portraits and Other Stories. *He lived in*
Bombay for two years before moving to London in 1970.
He spent four years in England and worked in
advertising, as well as writing for several literary
journals. He now lives in Sydney where he has recently
completed his first novel.

'Life of The Party' describes the entertaining and
intriguing story of a man who invites a number of
friends to a party at his house, a party at which he
doesn't appear himself; but he observes what happens
in his absence from the tree-house* built for his children
in the garden.

Please picture a pink gum-tree in the corner of a backyard.* This is a suburban gum sprouting more green in
the lower regions than usual, and a tree-house hammered into the first fork. A stunted* tree, but a note-
worthy one in our suburb. I live with my wife Joy and
two boys Geoffrey and Mark in a suburb of white
fences, lawns and tennis courts. It has its disadvantages.
On Sundays drivers persist in cruising* past, to peer and
comment as we tend* our gardens. I wonder what their

houses are like. Where do they live? Why do they drive around to see the work done by other citizens? Let me say I am concerned and curious about these things.

Last Sunday was a day of warm temperatures; pure pleasure, really. Tennis sounds filled my ears, and the whine of weekend lawnmowers. There was smoke from burning autumn leaves. I went down to the back of my yard, waited, looked around, and climbed to the tree-house.

I am forty-five years of age, in reasonable shape* all round. On Sundays I wear brown shorts. Still, it was a climb which was tricky in spots, and then as I settled down the house itself wobbled and creaked under my weight. The binoculars I placed on one of Geoffrey's nails; I moved my weight carefully; I surveyed my backyard and the squares of neighbouring houses. Half an hour remained before the party began.

On my left was Hedley's, the only flat roof for miles. He was out the front raking leaves. The sight of rubbish smoke billowing from that tin drum of his made me wonder at lack of thought. We had no washing on the line but was Hedley's act typical of a non-conformist,* the owner of a flat-roofed house? It was just a question. It reminded me of his car (a Fiat), his special brand of cigarettes, his hair which was slightly grey, and his wife, Zelda. Everything she did seemed to begin with Z. An odd game, but true. It was Zelda who owned the street's zaniest* laugh, had zealous opinions on the best-sellers,* and always said zero instead of the more normal nought or nothing.

In the next house I could see a tennis game. That accounted for the steady plok, plok and random shouts. I trained my glasses on the play without knowing the score. The antics of those people in slow distant motion were quite fantastic. To think that a wire box had been built to dart about in, to chase a small ball in, and shout.

That was George Watkins. As director of a profitable girdle* factory he has an inside story on human fitness. He's also a powerful surfer* and when I see him walking he shouts to me, 'How you going, Sid?'

The first time I played a game with big Watkins he aced* me and aced me in front of his friends and my wife. Invitations have been received since, but I miss the game to avoid additional embarrassment.

Across the street I could distinguish the drive and the side of Pollard's leafy yard. This is a Cape Cod* type of house. As expected Pollard was there, walking up the drive stopping at plants, hands in trousers, pausing, checking bricks, until he reached the footpath. There, he looked up and down, waiting for mail, visitors, his Prodigal Son, news of some description. He parades the width of his house, a balding figure with a jutting* stare like the house.

To my right a widow lives with her daughter. The street was alarmed when Gil died – he seemed to be as healthy as any of us. A short time after, she had a swimming pool dug and tiled and can be heard splashing during the days of hot temperature. From my position, as I waited, the waters were calm. Then I thought I saw a man there, lying beneath one of her pool trees, a solid hairy specimen, on one of those aluminium extension chairs. No? The glasses showed an image of some description. She is wearing slacks,* and is blonde and nervous.

Finally, there was the house next door on my right. The binoculars were hardly needed: I was looking down into the weedy garden, and as usual not a soul could be seen. These neighbours are the J. S. Yamas. In three years I suppose I have seen them . . . a dozen times. We have not spoken yet. He has nodded, yes, and smiled, but not spoken. This indifference deeply offends my wife.

'It's wrong the way they don't mix in!'*

'Why?'

'Everyone needs neighbours and friends. To talk to.'

'Why?'

'You can't live by yourself,' she says. 'What if something happens?'

That was her frustration as I remember it. Naturally enough, the Yamas's silence made them more and more discussed. The street kept its eyes open. Thinking about it: the Yamas have a private income; he could be a scholar of some sort; it could be, of course, that one of them is in shocking health, though I doubt it from what I sense of the place. He looks foreign, not Australian, and a fairly decent type.

At that time my yard was silent. Joy was at our beach-house with Geoffrey and Mark. I had said to them on Saturday night: 'Look, I have to duck up to* town tomorrow.' Arriving, I arranged the place and made for the tree-house. I had raised the venetians* and left the screen door open. We have lawn smoothing over most of our yard, and concrete blocks form a path. (I used to say that ours was a two-lawnmower house – one for the front and one for the back – until people took me seriously.) Halfway between the back door and the tree stands a permanent brick barbecue, tables and white chairs.

I had invited a dozen or so couples. On the tables I placed plenty of beer, glasses, knives and forks, serviettes, and under Joy's fly-proof net a stack of steaks, sausages and piles of bread rolls. Tell me a friend of yours who doesn't enjoy a barbecue on Sunday! From Geoffrey's tree-house I waited for the guests to arrive. Then a movement occurred on my left. A door slammed, a floral dress fluttered, down my drive came Norm Daniels and his wife. With the binoculars I caught their facial expressions. They began smiling. He adjusted his blue short-sleeved shirt as they neared the front door.

I waited. The Daniels now came around the house, puzzled by the no-answer at the front, seriously looking down the drive; certainly bewildered. Had they arrived on the wrong day? Then, of course, they turned and sighted the barbecue all laid out, and their relief was visible.

Daniels was monk-bald to me as I stared down. He waited among the tables as his wife called through the back door, 'You-who!' She smiled at the fly-screen, then shook her head at the tables and chairs.

'Not there?' Daniels asked.

'They must have gone out for a sec.'

He looked at his watch, settled back, and began eating one of my rolls. 'Want one?' he asked. She shook her hair. Surrounded by someone else's fresh meat and utensils, she seemed uncomfortable.

Another car pulled up. Daniels went over to the drive.

'Down the back!' he called out.

It was Lennie Maunder. About fifty, he was as soft as pork, wore bermuda shorts,* and had a bachelor's lopsided walk.

'No one's here,' Daniels explained. 'They must have gone out for a sec. I'm Norm Daniels. My wife, Joan. Pleased to meet yah.* We might as well hang around* till they get here.'

They sat down and I couldn't catch* all their words. It was a distraction trying to listen to them and watch for the next arrival. The word 'insurance' floated up to my tree, so I knew Daniels had started on occupations. They were not drinking at this stage, and when Frank and elegant Georgina Lloyd came down they seemed embarrassed, caught as it were, and stood up stiffly, bumping chairs, to smile.

Two more couples arrived, the men with bottles.

'Well,' Andy Cheel said, 'we might as well have a beer!'

Laughter. The sun was beaming. They began drinking.

The women were seated together, and pecked at the air like birds. I heard Frank Lloyd extroverting* into Sampson's ear. Tiny for his name, Sampson was in a bank somewhere, and accordingly grey.* Nodding, he said, 'This is right. This is right. Yes, this is right.'

Lloyd was in advertising and already into his third glass. He blew froth from the top of it. 'Ahhh,' he said, and half-closed his eyes.

The chairs were comfortable, the voices grew louder. Latecomers arrived. Norm Daniels and Lloyd realized they were friends of Ed Canning.

'Come over here, you bastard,' they said to him. Lloyd shouted, 'Who's the old bag* you've got with you?'

'Oh, you!' said Canning's wife. She was quite heavy, but pleased with Lloyd's compliment.

'Have a beer,' he said, 'Sid's not here yet.'

And Bill Smallacombe, who was climbing* at Myers, arriving without his wife.

I had a brief mental picture of Joy. In bed one night she sat up and said: 'I saw Bill Smallacombe at lunch today with a young girl.' She fell back disappointed, full of indignant thoughts; a brown-haired concerned wife is my Joy. As I watched the party I imagined Joy submitting to the sun on the sand, breasts flattened, lying there keeping an eye on* young Geoffrey and Mark. She must be satisfied with my career so far and is privately contented when I rush to town on business.

They were all there now, and the drinking had loosened muscles, floated the mouth muscles, wobbling the sincerities. The perils of Sunday afternoon drinking! Ed

Canning and Frank Lloyd had taken off their shirts, Lloyd's wife loosened her blouse buttons, familiar back-slapping occurred; laughter, so much laughter. I noticed the bachelor Maunder began stealing beer from someone else's glass. Bill Smallacombe drank heavily and kept going inside to use my lavatory. Clem Emery I could hear repeating the latest stock market prices, and Sampson was complaining that his new concrete path had been ruined overnight by a neighbour's dog.

'What say we get stuck into the grub?'* yelled Andy Cheel.

They all crowded forward, chewed on their words, dropping sauce and bones on the lawn, and briefly my name.

'Clear those bottles off the table, Ed, before they fall off,' said Canning's wife. She was wearing tight blue slacks.

Carrying four to each hand he lifted the bottles over legs, lawn, to dump them behind the garage. Two were dropped on the last load, and broke with an evil loudness. Someone called out, 'He dropped his bundle!' and they laughed and laughed.

Later, Ed's wife said, 'You should see their lounge!'*

'Those curtains I didn't like,' said Georgina Lloyd. 'I suppose Joy picked them.'

'I've been with her when she's bought stuff that really makes you wonder,' said Joan Daniels.

'Where do you think they got to,* anyway?' she asked vaguely.

By about half-past four the party was noisy. This was emphasized when the Watkins's tennis game suddenly stopped. And from the corner of my eye I caught grey-haired Hedley next door creeping towards our fence. I waited. Hedley squatted down, peered between the planks at the goings-on.* He hadn't shaved over the week-end, he twitched his nose, and at one stage

scratched between his legs. For a good fifteen minutes
Hedley spied before retreating. At his door he said
something to his wife, and they went inside. Directly
over the road, half-hidden by cars, George Pollard on
the footpath faced the direction of our house. The other
neighbours were either out or had decided to display no
interest at all.

'Only a few bottles left,' Cheel announced loudly.
'Sid's got Scotch inside, but we'd better not.'

'Why not?' asked Lloyd.

There was laughter at that, and I had to smile.

Lloyd touched Canning's wife on her behind. 'You
old bag,' he said. She allowed his arm to go around her
neck as he lit a cigarette.

Lloyd later tried a hand-stand* between two chairs,
tricky at his middle age, and swung off balance, knock-
ing chairs and breaking glasses. He landed on a pile of
chop bones; he lay there sweating, his chest heaving.

'When are you getting your pool?' Georgina asked
Clem Emery.

'Say seven weeks. We'll have a bit of a do* one night.'

'Yes, yes, don't forget us,' others shouted.

Then Smallacombe came wandering down to the
tree. He stopped right at the foot, kicked a tin, grunted,
and loudly urinated. The others glanced vaguely. Sampson turned, but it did seem natural enough, relieving
yourself against a gum-tree on a Sunday afternoon.

Frank Lloyd, trying to balance a bottle on the hairs of
one arm, was pulled away by his wife. 'Come on, darl.*
We must be off.'* She called to the rest, 'We'll be seeing
you.'

'Gawd,* it's twenty past six.'

The Daniels moved out with the Lloyds.

'What about this mess?'

'She'll be right.'

Smallacombe belched.

'Leave it.'

My tree was draughty. They had me bored. I wanted them to go, to leave my place. Why do they linger, sitting about?

Gradually they gathered sunglasses, car keys, their cardigans and handbags, and drifted up the drive in a sad fashion as if they were leaving a beach.

At the gate Ed Canning stopped and shouted, 'I've never been so drunk in all my life!' It was a voice of announcement, sincere, and clearly loud enough to reach my tree. My binoculars showed middle-aged, sun-glassed Canning rigid with seriousness after his statement. Canning, the manager saving for boat and beach-house; his wife had begun yoga classes.

Finally, there was the accelerating procession of shining sedans, saloons, station-wagons, stretching past my house. Most of them I noticed had tow bars* fitted. Canning, Smallacombe, Cheel, Emery, Sampson, Maunder, etc. One of them sounded his horn three, four times in passing. Was it Smallacombe? He was one of my friends. A stillness occurred, a familiar hour was beginning, lights flickered. And sliding down the tree I had to think about: who would have sounded his horn at me?

Glossary

page 105
tree-house: miniature house built in a tree
backyard: open area behind and belonging to a house
stunted: small, not well developed
cruising: driving slowly and leisurely
tend: look after, work in

page 106
shape: physical condition
non-conformist: person who refuses to behave in the usually accepted way

zaniest: craziest, most unusual
best-sellers: books which sell in very large numbers

page 107
girdle: a sort of wide belt worn round the waist to make one
    look slimmer
surfer: person practising the sport of riding on a wooden
    board on the surface of the sea's waves (very popular in
    Australia)
aced: played an unreturnable tennis serve
Cape Cod: a place on the north-east coast of the U.S.A. in the
    state of Massachusetts
jutting: sticking out
slacks: trousers for casual, leisure wear
mix in: to be sociable

page 108
duck up to: make a brief, unexpected visit
venetians: sunblinds usually made of narrow, horizontal strips
    of plastic

page 109
bermuda shorts: knee-length sports trousers
yah: (slang) you
hang around: wait
catch: hear, understand

page 110
extroverting: talking loudly and sociably
grey: dull, colourless personality
old bag: (slang) ugly (old) woman
climbing: on his way towards a senior position in the company
keeping an eye on: watching to see the children don't get into
    any trouble

page 111
get stuck into the grub: (slang) start eating the food
lounge: main living-room
they got to: where they are
goings-on: noisy activity

114

page 112
hand-stand: to stand upside down, on his hands
a bit of a do: a small party
darl (= darling)
be off: go, leave
Gawd: (slang) God, an expression of surprise

page 113
tow bar(s): attachment for pulling a caravan on the back of a
   car

Questions

1 What did the narrator do before his guests arrived?
2 What particularly makes the Yamas family different from
   the other people who live near the narrator's house?
3 What is the narrator's name? How do we know this?
4 How did the various neighbours who were not invited
   react to the party?
5 What was the narrator's reaction as the guests began to
   leave?
6 Describe the narrator's house and garden as fully as you
   can.
7 What sort of person does the story suggest the narrator is?

Topics for discussion

1 'Why do they drive around to see the work done by other
   citizens?' (page 106). What is your answer to this question?
2 In what ways does your home town and its atmosphere
   differ from that described here?
3 In what ways do you see this as a particularly Australian
   story? In what ways one that could have taken place
   anywhere?
4 On page 106 the narrator describes his reaction to tennis.
   What sport(s) make(s) you react in a similar way?
5 'It's wrong the way they don't mix in!'
   'Why?'
   'Everyone needs neighbours and friends. To talk to' (page
108). How far do you think the narrator's wife is right here?

6 Which of the characters in the story do you particularly like (or dislike)?

7 Why do you think the narrator decided to observe the party from the tree-house? How would you summarize his observations?

8 How do you think you would react if you were invited to a party and found the people who had invited you were not there?

Frank O'Connor
The Genius

*Frank O'Connor, whose real name was Michael
O'Donovan, was born in Cork, in the south-west of
Ireland in 1903. O'Connor was very largely self-
educated and began to prepare the first collected edition
of his own work when he was only twelve. Later he
worked as a librarian, translator and journalist, and
always had a very strong interest in the Irish language
and the literature and music of his Celtic ancestors. His
poems and translations were first published in the
magazine* Irish Statesman *and he also built up a
considerable reputation as a theatre director in Ireland.
Frank O'Connor published his first book,* Quest of the
Nation *in 1931 and from then until his death in 1966
wrote more than 30 volumes – mainly of short stories
and plays, set against the background of his native
Ireland.
This story is taken from his well-known collection called*
My Oedipus Complex and Other Stories (*1953*) *and
charmingly describes the growing up pains of a young
Irish boy who feels his fate in life is to be a genius.*

Some kids are cissies* by nature but I was a cissy by
conviction. Mother had told me about geniuses; I
wanted to be one, and I could see for myself that fighting, as well as being sinful, was dangerous. The kids
round the Barrack where I lived were always fighting.
Mother said they were savages, that I needed proper

friends, and that once I was old enough to go to school I would meet them.

My way, when someone wanted to fight and I could not get away, was to climb on the nearest wall and argue like hell in a shrill voice about Our Blessed Lord and good manners. This was a way of attracting attention, and it usually worked because the enemy, having stared incredulously at me for several minutes, wondering if he would have time to hammer my head on the pavement before someone came out to him, yelled something like 'blooming* cissy' and went away in disgust. I didn't like being called a cissy but I preferred it to fighting. I felt very like one of those poor mongrels* who slunk through our neighbourhood and took to their heels* when anyone came near them, and I always tried to make friends with them.

I toyed with* games, and enjoyed kicking a ball gently before me along the pavement till I discovered that any boy who joined me grew violent and started to shoulder me out of the way. I preferred little girls because they didn't fight so much, but otherwise I found them insipid and lacking in any solid basis of information. The only women I cared for* were grown-ups, and my most intimate friend was an old washerwoman called Miss Cooney who had been in the lunatic asylum and was very religious. It was she who had told me all about dogs. She would run a mile after anyone she saw hurting an animal, and even went to the police about them, but the police knew she was mad and paid no attention.

She was a sad-looking woman with grey hair, high cheek-bones and toothless gums. While she ironed, I would sit for hours in the hot, steaming, damp kitchen, turning over the pages of her religious books. She was fond of me too, and told me she was sure I would be a priest. I agreed that I might be a bishop, but she didn't seem to think so highly of bishops. I told her there were so many other things I might be that I couldn't make up my mind, but she only smiled at this. Miss Cooney thought there was only one thing a genius could be and that was a priest.

On the whole I thought an explorer was what I would be. Our house was in a square between two roads, one terraced above the other, and I could leave home, follow the upper road for a mile past the Barrack, turn left on any of the intervening roads and lanes, and return almost without leaving the pavement. It was astonishing what valuable information you could pick up* on a trip like that. When I came home I wrote down my adventures in a book called *The Voyages of Johnson Martin*, 'with many Maps and Illustrations, Irishtown University Press, 3s. 6d. nett'. I was also compiling *The Irishtown University Song Book for Use in Schools and Institutions by Johnson Martin,* which had the words and music of my favourite songs. I could not read music yet but I copied it from anything that came handy, preferring staff* to solfa* because it looked better on the page. But I still wasn't sure what I would be. All I knew was that I intended to be famous and have a statue put up to me near that of Father Matthew, in Patrick Street. Father Matthew was called the Apostle of Temperance,* but I didn't think much of* temperance. So far our town hadn't a proper genius and I intended to supply the deficiency.

But my work continued to bring home to me* the great gaps in my knowledge. Mother understood my difficulty and worried herself endlessly finding answers to my questions, but neither she nor Miss Cooney had a great store of the sort of information I needed, and Father was more a hindrance than a help. He was talkative enough about subjects that interested himself but they did not greatly interest me. 'Ballybeg,' he would say brightly. 'Market town. Population 648. Nearest

station. Rathkeale.' He was also forthcoming enough
about other things, but later, Mother would take me
aside and explain that he was only joking again. This
made me mad, because I never knew when he was joking
and when he wasn't.

I can see now, of course, that he didn't really like me.
It was not the poor man's fault. He had never expected
to be the father of a genius and it filled him with fore-
bodings. He looked round him at all his contemporaries
who had normal, blood-thirsty, illiterate children, and
shuddered at the thought that I would never be good
for anything but being a genius. To give him his due,*
it wasn't himself he worried about, but there had never
been anything like it in the family before and he dreaded
the shame of it. He would come in from the front door
with his cap over his eyes and his hands in his trouser
pockets and stare moodily at me while I sat at the kitchen
table, surrounded by papers, producing fresh maps and
illustrations for my book of voyages, or copying the
music of 'The Minstrel Boy'.

'Why can't you go out and play with the Horgans?'
he would ask wheedlingly, trying to make it sound
attractive.

'I don't like the Horgans, Daddy,' I would reply
politely.

'But what's wrong with them?' he would ask testily.
'They're fine manly young fellows.'

'They're always fighting, Daddy.'

'And what harm is fighting? Can't you fight them
back?'

'I don't like fighting, Daddy, thank you,' I would say,
still with perfect politeness.

'The dear knows, the child is right,' Mother would
say, coming to my defence. 'I don't know what sort
those children are.'

'Ah, you have him as bad as yourself,' Father would

snort, and stalk to the front door again, to scald his heart
with thoughts of the nice natural son he might have had
if only he hadn't married the wrong woman. Granny
had always said Mother was the wrong woman for him
and now she was being proved right.

She was being proved so right that the poor man
couldn't keep his eyes off me, waiting for the insanity to
break out in me. One of the things he didn't like was my
Opera House. The Opera House was a cardboard box I
had mounted on two chairs in the dark hallway. It had a
proscenium* cut in it, and I had painted some back-
drops* of mountain and sea, with wings* that represen-
ted trees and rocks. The characters were pictures cut
out, mounted and coloured, and moved on bits of stick.
It was lit with candles, for which I had made coloured
screens, greased so that they were transparent, and I
made up operas from story-books and bits of songs. I
was singing a passionate duet for two of the characters
while twiddling the screens to produce the effect of
moonlight when one of the screens caught fire and
everything went up in a mass of flames. I screamed and
Father came out to stamp out the blaze, and he cursed
me till even Mother lost her temper with him and told
him he was worse than six children, after which he
wouldn't speak to her for a week.

Another time I was so impressed with a lame* teacher
I knew that I decided to have a lame leg myself, and
there was hell in the home for days because Mother had
no difficulty at all in seeing that my foot was already out
of shape while Father only looked at it and sniffed con-
temptuously. I was furious with him, and Mother decided he wasn't much better than a monster. They
quarrelled for days over that until it became quite an
embarrassment to me because, though I was bored stiff*
with limping, I felt I should be letting her down* by
getting better. When I went down the Square, lurching

from side to side, Father stood at the gate, looking after me with a malicious knowing smile, and when I had discarded my limp, the way he mocked Mother was positively disgusting.

As I say, they squabbled* endlessly about what I should be told. Father was for telling me nothing.

'But, Mick,' Mother would say earnestly, 'the child must learn.'

'He'll learn soon enough when he goes to school,' he snarled. 'Why do you be always at him, putting ideas into his head? Isn't he bad enough? I'd sooner* the boy would grow up a bit natural.'

But either Mother didn't like children to be natural or she thought I was natural enough as I was. Women, of course, don't object to geniuses half as much as men do. I suppose they find them a relief.

Now one of the things I wanted badly to know was where babies came from, but this was something that no one seemed to be able to explain to me. When I asked Mother she got upset and talked about birds and flowers, and I decided that if she had ever known she must have forgotten it and was ashamed to say so. Miss Cooney only smiled wistfully when I asked her and said, 'You'll know all about it soon enough, child.'

'But, Miss Cooney,' I said with great dignity, 'I have to know now. It's for my work, you see.'

'Keep your innocence while you can, child,' she said in the same tone. 'Soon enough the world will rob you of it, and once 'tis gone 'tis gone for ever.'

But whatever the world wanted to rob me of, it was welcome to it from my point of view, if only I could get a few facts to work on.* I appealed to Father and he told me that babies were dropped out of aeroplanes and if you caught one you could keep it. 'By parachute?' I asked, but he only looked pained and said, 'Oh, no, you don't want to begin by spoiling them.' Afterwards, Mother took me aside again and explained that he was only joking. I went quite dotty* with rage and told her that one of these days he would go too far with his jokes.

All the same, it was a great worry to Mother. It wasn't every mother who had a genius for a son, and she dreaded that she might be wronging me. She suggested timidly to Father that he should tell me something about it and he danced with rage. I heard them because I was supposed to be playing with the Opera House upstairs at the time. He said she was going out of her mind, and that she was driving me out of my mind at the same time. She was very upset because she had considerable respect for his judgement.

At the same time when it was a matter of duty she could be very, very obstinate. It was a heavy responsibility, and she disliked it intensely – a deeply pious woman who never mentioned the subject at all to anybody if she could avoid it – but it had to be done. She took an awful long time over it – it was a summer day, and we were sitting on the bank of a stream in the Glen – but at last I managed to detach the fact that mummies had an engine in their tummies* and daddies had a starting-handle that made it work, and once it started it went on until it made a baby. That certainly explained an awful lot of things I had not understood up to this – for instance, why fathers were necessary and why Mother had buffers* on her chest while Father had none. It made her almost as interesting as a locomotive,* and for days I went round deploring my own rotten luck that I wasn't a girl and couldn't have an engine and buffers of my own instead of a measly* old starting handle like Father.

Soon afterwards I went to school and disliked it intensely. I was too small to be moved up to the big boys and the other 'infants' were still at the stage of spelling

Frank O'Connor

'cat' and 'dog'. I tried to tell the old teacher about my work, but she only smiled and said, 'Hush, Larry!' I hated being told to hush. Father was always saying it to me.

One day I was standing at the playground gate, feeling very lonely and dissatisfied, when a tall girl from the Senior Girls' school spoke to me. She was a girl with a plump, dark face and black pigtails.*

'What's your name, little boy?' she asked.

I told her.

'Is this your first time at school?' she asked.

'Yes.'

'And do you like it?'

'No, I hate it,' I replied gravely. 'The children can't spell and the old woman talks too much.'

Then I talked myself for a change and she listened attentively while I told her about myself, my voyages, my books and the time of the trains from all the city stations. As she seemed so interested I told her I would meet her after school and tell her some more.

I was as good as my word. When I had eaten my lunch, instead of going on further voyages I went back to the Girls' School and waited for her to come out. She seemed pleased to see me because she took my hand and brought me home with her. She lived up Gardiner's Hill, a steep, demure* suburban road with trees that overhung the walls at either side. She lived in a small house on top of the hill and was one of a family of three girls. Her little brother, John Joe, had been killed the previous year by a car. 'Look at what I brought home with me!' she said when we went into the kitchen, and her mother, a tall, thin woman made a great fuss* of me and wanted me to have my dinner with Una. That was the girl's name. I didn't take anything, but while she ate I sat by the range* and told her mother about myself as well. She seemed to like it as much as Una, and when

124

dinner was over Una took me out in the fields behind
the house for a walk.

When I went home at teatime, Mother was delighted.

'Ah,' she said, 'I knew you wouldn't be long making
nice friends at school. It's about time for you, the dear
knows.'

I felt much the same about it, and every fine day at
three I waited for Una outside the school. When it
rained and Mother would not let me out I was mis-
erable.

One day while I was waiting for her there were two
senior girls outside the gate.

'Your girl isn't out yet, Larry,' said one with a giggle.

'And do you mean to tell me Larry has a girl?' the
other asked with a shocked air.

'Oh, yes,' said the first. 'Una Dwyer is Larry's girl. He
goes with Una, don't you, Larry?'

I replied politely that I did, but in fact I was seriously
alarmed. I had not realized that Una would be considered my girl. It had never happened to me before,
and I had not understood that my waiting for her would
be regarded in such a grave light. Now, I think the girls
were probably right anyhow, for that is always the way
it has happened to me. A woman has only to shut up and
let me talk long enough for me to fall head and ears* in
love with her. But then I did not recognize the symptoms. All I knew was that going with somebody meant
you intended to marry them. I had always planned on
marrying Mother; now it seemed as if I was expected to
marry someone else, and I wasn't sure if I should like it
or, if, like football, it would prove to be one of those
games that two people could not play without pushing.

A couple of weeks later I went to a party at Una's
house. By this time it was almost as much mine as theirs.
All the girls liked me and Mrs Dwyer talked to me by
the hour.* I saw nothing peculiar about this except a

125

proper appreciation of geniuses. Una had warned me
that I should be expected to sing, so I was ready for the
occasion. I sang the Gregorian *Credo*, and some of the
little girls laughed, but Mrs Dwyer only looked at me
fondly.

'I suppose you'll be a priest when you grow up,
Larry?' she asked.

'No, Mrs Dwyer,' I replied firmly. 'As a matter of fact
I intend to be a composer. Priests can't marry, you see,
and I want to get married.'

That seemed to surprise her quite a bit. I was quite
prepared to continue discussing my plans for the future,
but all the children talked together. I was used to planning discussions so that they went on for a long time, but
I found that whenever I began one in the Dwyers', it
was immediately interrupted so that I found it hard to
concentrate. Besides, all the children shouted, and Mrs
Dwyer, for all her gentleness, shouted with them and at
them. At first, I was somewhat alarmed, but I soon saw
that they meant no particular harm, and when the party
ended I was jumping up and down on the sofa, shrieking
louder than anyone while Una, in hysterics of giggling,
encouraged me. She seemed to think I was the funniest
thing ever.

It was a moonlit November night, and lights were
burning in the little cottages along the road when Una
brought me home. On the road outside she stopped uncertainly and said, 'This is where little John Joe was
killed.'

There was nothing remarkable about the spot, and I
saw no chance of acquiring any useful information.

'Was it a Ford or a Morris?' I asked, more out of
politeness than anything else.

'I don't know,' she replied with smouldering anger. 'It
was Donegan's old car. They can never look where
they're going, the old shows!'*

'Our Lord probably wanted him,' I said perfunctorily.

'I dare say* He did,' Una replied, though she showed no particular conviction. 'That old fool, Donegan – I could kill him whenever I think of it.'

'You should get your mother to make you another,' I suggested helpfully.

'Make me a what?' Una exclaimed in consternation.

'Make you another brother,' I repeated earnestly. 'It's quite easy, really. She has an engine in her tummy, and all your daddy has to do is to start it with his starting-handle.'

'Cripes!'* Una said, and clapped her hand over her mouth in an explosion of giggles. 'Imagine me telling her that!'

'But it's true, Una,' I said obstinately. 'It only takes nine months. She could make you another little brother by next summer.'

'Oh, Jay!' exclaimed Una in another fit of giggles. 'Who told you all that?'

'Mummy did. Didn't your mother tell you?'

'Oh, she says you buy them from Nurse Daly,' said Una, and began to giggle again.

'I wouldn't really believe that,' I said with as much dignity as I could muster.*

But the truth was I felt I had made a fool of myself again. I realized now that I had never been convinced by Mother's explanation. It was too simple. If there was anything that woman could get wrong she did without fail. And it upset me, because for the first time I found myself wanting to make a really good impression. The Dwyers had managed to convince me that whatever else I wanted to be I did not want to be a priest. I didn't even want to be an explorer, a career which would take me away for long periods from my wife and family. I was prepared to be a composer and nothing but a composer. That night in bed I sounded* Mother on the subject of marriage. I tried to be tactful because it had always been agreed between us that I should marry her and I did not wish her to see that my feelings had changed.

'Mummy,' I asked, 'If a gentleman asks a lady to marry him, what does he say?'

'Oh,' she replied shortly, 'some of them say a lot. They say more than they mean.'

She was so irritable that I guessed she had divined my secret and I felt really sorry for her.

'If a gentleman said, "Excuse me, will you marry me?" would that be all right?' I persisted.

'Ah, well, he'd have to tell her first that he was fond of her,' said Mother who, no matter what she felt, could never bring herself* to deceive me on any major issue.

But about the other matter I saw that it was hopeless to ask her any more. For days I made the most pertinacious inquiries at school and received some startling information. One boy had actually come floating down on a snowflake, wearing a bright blue dress, but to his chagrin* and mine, the dress had been given away to a poor child in the North Main Street. I grieved long and deeply over this wanton* destruction of evidence. The balance of opinion favoured Mrs Dwyer's solution, but of the theory of engines and starting-handles no one in the school had ever heard. That theory might have been all right when Mother was a girl but it was now definitely out of fashion.

And because of it I had been exposed to ridicule before the family whose good opinion I valued most. It was hard enough to keep up my dignity with a girl who was doing algebra while I hadn't got beyond long division without falling into childish errors that made her laugh. That is another thing I still cannot stand, being made fun of by women. Once they begin on it they never stop. Once when we were going up Gardiner's Hill together after school she stopped to look at a baby in a pram. The baby grinned at her and she gave him her finger to suck. He waved his fists and sucked like mad,* and she went off into giggles again.

'I suppose that was another engine?' she said.

Four times at least she mentioned my silliness, twice in front of other girls and each time, though I pretended to ignore it, I was pierced to the heart. It made me determined not to be exposed again. Once Mother asked Una and her younger sister, Joan, to tea, and all the time I was in an agony of self-consciousness, dreading what she would say next. I felt that a woman who had said such things about babies was capable of anything. Then the talk turned on the death of little John Joe, and it all flowed back into my mind on a wave of mortification. I made two efforts to change the conversation, but Mother returned to it. She was full of pity for the Dwyers, full of sympathy for the little boy and had almost reduced herself to tears. Finally I got up and ordered Una and Joan to play with me. Then Mother got angry.

'For goodness' sake, Larry, let the children finish their tea!' she snapped.

'It's all right, Mrs Delaney,' Una said good-naturedly. 'I'll go with him.'

'Nonsense, Una!' Mother said sharply. 'Finish your tea and go on with what you were saying. It's a wonder to me your poor mother didn't go out of her mind. How can they let people like that drive cars?'

At this I set up a loud wail.* At any moment now I felt she was going to get on to babies and advise Una about what her mother ought to do.

'Will you behave yourself, Larry!' Mother said in a quivering voice. 'Or what's come over you* in the past few weeks? You used to have such nice manners, and now look at you! A little corner boy!* I'm ashamed of you!'

How could she know what had come over me? How could she realize that I was imagining the family circle in the Dwyers' house and Una, between fits of laughter, describing my old-fashioned mother who still talked about babies coming out of people's stomachs? It must have been real love, for I have never known true love in which I wasn't ashamed of Mother.

And she knew it and was hurt. I still enjoyed going home with Una in the afternoons and while she ate her dinner, I sat at the piano and pretended to play my own compositions, but whenever she called at our house for me I grabbed her by the hand and tried to drag her away so that she and Mother shouldn't start talking.

'Ah, I'm disgusted with you,' Mother said one day. 'One would think you were ashamed of me in front of that little girl. I'll engage* she doesn't treat her mother like that.'

Then one day I was waiting for Una at the school gate as usual. Another boy was waiting there as well – one of the seniors. When he heard the screams of the school breaking up* he strolled away and stationed himself at the foot of the hill by the crossroads. Then Una herself came rushing out in her wide-brimmed felt hat, swinging her satchel,* and approached me with a conspiratorial air.

'Oh, Larry, guess what's happened!' she whispered. 'I can't bring you home with me today. I'll come down and see you during the week though. Will that do?'

'Yes, thank you,' I said in a dead cold voice. Even at the most tragic moment of my life I could be nothing but polite. I watched her scamper* down the hill to where the big boy was waiting. He looked over his shoulder with a grin, and then the two of them went off together.

Instead of following them I went back up the hill alone and stood leaning over the quarry wall, looking at the roadway and the valley of the city beneath me. I knew this was the end. I was too young to marry Una. I didn't know where babies came from and I didn't understand algebra. The fellow she had gone home with probably knew everything about both. I was full of gloom and revengeful thoughts. I, who had considered it sinful and dangerous to fight, was now regretting that I hadn't gone after him to batter his teeth in and jump on his face. It wouldn't have mattered to me that I was too young and weak and that he would have done all the battering. I saw that love was a game that two people couldn't play at without pushing, just like football.

I went home and, without saying a word, took out the work I had been neglecting so long. That too seemed to have lost its appeal. Moodily I ruled five lines and began to trace the difficult sign of the treble clef.*

'Didn't you see Una, Larry?' Mother asked in surprise, looking up from her sewing.

'No, Mummy,' I said, too full for speech.

'Wisha, 'twasn't a falling-out ye had?'* she asked in dismay, coming towards me. I put my head on my hands and sobbed. 'Wisha, never mind childeen!'* she murmured, running her hand through my hair. 'She was a bit old for you. You reminded her of her little brother that was killed, of course – that was why. You'll soon make new friends, take my word for it.'

But I did not believe her. That evening there was no comfort for me. My great work meant nothing to me and I knew it was all I would ever have. For all the difference it made I might as well become a priest. I felt it was a poor, sad, lonesome thing being nothing but a genius.

Glossary

page 117
cissies: people who are afraid of things, having no courage

page 118
blooming: (slang) a weak word for the swear word 'bloody'
mongrels: dogs of mixed breeding
took to their heels: ran away
toyed with: took an interest in but didn't consider seriously
cared for: liked

page 119
pick up: collect
staff: staves, a set of lines and spaces on which music is written
solfa: the notes of a musical scale
Temperance: moderation – here in the sense of drinking no
    alcohol
didn't think much of: had very little respect for
bring home to me: made me realize

page 120
to give him his due: to be fair to him

page 121
proscenium: the stage in a classically built theatre
back-drops: large pieces of material providing the scenery at
    the back of the stage
wings: the sides of a stage where the actors make their
    entrances and exits
lame: disabled in one or both legs
bored stiff: absolutely bored
letting her down: not fulfilling his obligation to his mother

page 122
squabbled: argued (like children)
I'd sooner: I would prefer
work on: use as a basis for further investigation

page 123
dotty: mad
tummies: stomachs

buffers: literally, protection against shock, as on a train, here,
    referring to his mother's breasts
locomotive: train
measly: pathetic, uninteresting

page 124
pigtails: long twisted lengths of hair hanging down the
    back
demure: modest, unspectacular
made a great fuss: paid a great deal of attention, was very
    kind
range: an old-fashioned cooking stove

page 125
head and ears: completely
by the hour: for a very long time

page 126
old shows: literally 'show-offs', people full of boastful
    pretences

page 127
dare say: expect
cripes: a child's exclamation of great surprise and often of
    horror
muster: collect together, manage

page 128
sounded: asked questions
bring herself: allow, persuade herself
chagrin: annoyance (bad temper)
wanton: irresponsible, wasteful

page 129
like mad: with great energy and enthusiasm
wail: cry of sorrow and pain
come over you: made you behave in this awful way

page 130
a little corner boy: rude, like all the common children in the
    street

Frank O'Connor

I'll engage: I am sure
breaking up: the children ending their lessons for the day
satchel: school bag for carrying books and pencils etc.
scamper: run quickly

page 131
clef: the sign at the beginning of a line of music
wisha, 'twasn't a falling-out ye had? (dialect): I hope you
    didn't have an argument, did you?
childeen (a term of affection): child

Questions

1 What did other people think Larry would be when he grew
   up?
2 Why didn't Larry want to be what other people expected
   him to be?
3 What did Larry himself decide he would be when grown
   up?
4 Why did Larry dislike school?
5 What for Larry was different about the Dwyer family?
6 What role did Miss Cooney play in Larry's life?
7 Why was Larry so against his mother talking to Una?
8 What in the end made Larry feel there was perhaps some
   purpose in fighting other boys?
9 Describe Larry's mother as fully as you can.

Topics for discussion

1 How old do you think Larry was? Give reasons from the
   story to support your answer.
2 Why do you think Larry felt he was a genius? Is there any
   evidence in the story that he was mistaken in the belief?
3 Describe Larry's home background as fully as you can.
4 How far do you think Larry's mother was right in saying
   Una had given him up on account of the difference in their
   ages? Were there other reasons?
5 What evidence is there in the story of Larry's confidence in
   himself? How attractive a characteristic do you find this?

6 'Women, of course, don't object to geniuses half as much as men do' (page 122). To what extent do you think this is true?

7 'I saw that love was a game that two people couldn't play at without pushing, just like football' (page 131). How accurate do you feel this is?

Printed in the United States
By Bookmasters